"I stand in the Gorbals and before the world as a Bolshevik, alias a Communist, alias a revolutionary, alias a Marxist. My symbol is the red flag, and I shall always keep it flying high."

John Maclean, *Election Address*, November 1922

About the author

Dave Sherry is a public sector housing worker in Glasgow and a trade union activist for 40 years. He is the author of *Occupy! A Short History of Workers' Occupations* (Bookmarks 2010) and *Empire and Revolution: The Meaning of the First World War* (Bookmarks 2014). He is a member of the Socialist Workers Party.

JOHN MACLEAN:
RED CLYDESIDER

Dave Sherry

Bookmarks Publications

John Maclean: Red Clydesider
Dave Sherry
First published in 1998 by SWP
This edition published 2014 by Bookmarks Publications
c/o 1 Bloomsbury Street, London WC1B 3QE
© Bookmarks Publications
Cover design by Bookmarks Publications
Typeset by Bookmarks Publications
Printed by Halstan Printing Group
ISBN 978 1 909026 66 7

Contents

Introduction to the new edition   7

1   Maclean's significance   15

2   Britain and the age of empire   20

3   Becoming a socialist   23

4   A model social democrat   31

5   The outbreak of war   40

6   War on two fronts   45

7   The limits of trade unionism   55

8   The end of tsarism   66

9   The post-war storm   72

10   The retreat: Maclean and the CPGB   82

11   Socialist or nationalist?   87

Notes   94

Introduction to the new edition

The first edition of this pamphlet was published by *Socialist Worker* in 1998—the 75th anniversary of John Maclean's death. It has been out of print for some time and much has changed since it first appeared. In 1998 the Blair government was less than a year old and most labour voters still clung to the sentiment of the party's election anthem "Things can only get better". After 18 years of Thatcherism it seemed a reasonable expectation but instead, for most of us, things only got worse.

As I argued at the time, the writing was already on the wall:

> The millions who voted in May 1997 for real change have seen their hopes betrayed. Under Tony Blair and Gordon Brown, New Labour has embraced the market and governs in the interest of the rich. The leaders of the SNP are no different; they too are courting millionaire businessmen. Yet the market economy is plunging the whole world deeper into economic recession, military conflict and social upheaval. This is the real meaning of globalisation. The 20th century is set to end as it began—as Lenin said we are living in an epoch of wars and revolution.[1]

The start of the new century was accompanied by the rise of the mass anti-war movement and waves of political radicalisation directed at capitalism itself. Blair's slavish acceptance of the Bush Doctrine led to a permanent "war on terror" and the destabilising of the Middle East at a cost of trillions. Gordon Brown's embrace of neoliberalism and his devil pact with the City of London helped bring about the 2008 financial crash, ushering in the worst ever world recession.

These are desperate times. The tiny minority of super-rich, who created this mess, are trying to force the rest of us to pay for it. In response we have seen a rising wave of struggle against austerity throughout Europe and across the globe—including mass strikes, riots, the rise of the occupy movement and a series of Arab uprisings, culminating in the Egyptian Revolution beginning in January 2011.

The independence referendum and the legacy of John Maclean

2014 sees the anniversary of the First World War, the independence referendum and the hosting of the Commonwealth Games in Glasgow. The convergence of these three important events affords socialists an opportunity to shape the referendum campaign and challenge both British and Scottish nationalism.

Glasgow's merchants prospered from slavery and colonialism. Its street names—Jamaica, Virginia, Buchanan and Glassford—pay tribute to the plantation colonies and the Glasgow merchants who made vast fortunes in trading with them. These ill-gotten gains laid the basis for Glasgow's emergence as the British Empire's second city, when it became the key munitions hub for the British state and its war profiteers; together they bear collective responsibility for the slaughter of millions on the western front during the First World War.

Against the attempts of the state to whitewash militarism and colonialism in 2014 stands the tradition of the Red Clyde. In John Maclean, Glasgow produced an outstanding revolutionary leader who led the opposition to the First World War because he understood it as a war to repartition the world between the Great Powers, and that it would lead to further imperialist conflict involving the new global power, the United States.

He also grasped the importance of national liberation struggles in the colonies and how they could weaken the

British Empire and imperialism as a whole. This was manifested in his consistent support for the republican struggle in Ireland, Britain's oldest colony. In doing so Maclean was breaking from the dominant position of the British socialist movement.

The independence referendum will be at the centre of official politics in Scotland until the autumn of 2014, and it is vital that we connect it with the fight against austerity and the struggle for a better world. This pamphlet has been reprinted to assist in that process.

The Socialist Workers Party (SWP) has always supported Scotland's right to self-determination because socialists have no interest in defending the unity of the British state. But we have not previously argued that Scots must actively exercise their right to separate. Scotland is not an oppressed nation and, until recently, self-determination remained an abstract argument. But ever since it became clear that there will be a referendum, members of the SWP in Scotland have been campaigning for a yes vote, essentially for the following reasons:

○ The UK is an imperialist power that pillages the world's resources. It is a state at war in the Middle East, operating in alliance with US imperialism. It supported the invasions of Iraq and Afghanistan and is still willing to intervene in Syria and Iran. Prime minister Cameron and Labour leader Miliband are both desperate to preserve the union because a yes vote in the referendum will weaken the British state and make it more difficult to play the role of America's henchman. Calling for the breakup of Britain therefore means that independence can be supported for anti-imperialist reasons, without lining up behind the Scottish Nationalist Party (SNP).

○ The unionist campaign endorses a reactionary idea of Britishness based on imperialism, racism and anti-immigrant hysteria. Its backers will use the First World War centenary and Glasgow's hosting of the Commonwealth Games to spread propaganda about a glorious imperial past. The dominant tone of the "better together" campaign will not be the unity of the British working class, which should not be confused with the unity of the British state. It will not be about the Chartists, the Suffragettes or the Great Miners' Strike, and for socialists to give left wing cover to the pro-union campaign would be a grave mistake. If we fail to put forward an argument for class politics within the independence campaign, the choice will be British or Scottish nationalism. Evading the issue by abstaining is to opt for the former while pretending to oppose both.

○ With devolution has come the delegating of responsibility for cuts and austerity. If nothing else, in a separate state the Scottish government could no longer pass the buck to Westminster. In 2010, for example, the SNP cabinet "reluctantly" accepted the Tories' savage cut to its block grant funding from Westminster. Alex Salmond argued that the unprecedented 35 percent cut he made to the Scottish social housing budget was not as bad as the 65 percent cut to housing in England and Wales.

What kind of Scotland?

Socialists need to engage with all those who see the referendum as an opportunity to win something better than what's on offer from the SNP—including those who presently favour more devolved powers but can't vote for that option because it won't be on their ballot paper.

The political ramifications of what a future Scotland might look like are already upon us. The SNP leadership's decision to dump its most popular policy and keep an independent Scotland in Nato was a major turning point in the debate on independence. It underlines the need for a serious socialist position that won't accommodate to the nationalist project.

Although, under Salmond's leadership, the SNP has sought to claim the mantle of social democracy and win disillusioned Labour voters, in practice the SNP remains committed to a pro-business agenda. In 2012 Salmond was damaged by revelations about his close relationship with Rupert Murdoch. The *Sun* newspaper had backed him and the SNP, and it later emerged that he had met with Murdoch and, like Tory cabinet member Jeremy Hunt, promised to back his bid to gain total control over BSkyB.

The SNP's commitment to a capitalist Scotland has been clear from its very first budget. Money was spent ensuring business rates went down—hitting local authority services. Last year SNP finance minister John Swinney said he was "providing all the support we can to the business community", and boasted that "Scotland has the most competitive business rates in the UK".[2] Before the financial crash Salmond, a former economist with the Royal Bank of Scotland, cited his old bank as an example of what a great Scottish-based institution could achieve. He argued that Scotland could join "the arc of prosperity" with Iceland and Ireland, and become another "Celtic Tiger". In plain language this means a low wage economy competing with other low wage economies in a race to the bottom.

The existence of a Scottish national identity is not in question and there is no reason why Scotland could not become a capitalist nation state like any other. It is hypocritical to oppose Scottish nationalism and claim that it is reactionary, while remaining silent about British nationalism or, even worse, championing it. British nationalism is the main enemy, but we should be under no illusions about what kind of Scotland the SNP has in mind. It wants to retain the royal family, sterling, the Bank of England and Nato. It is a single-issue party, intent on achieving independence and nothing else.

Edinburgh-born socialist James Connolly—a contemporary of John Maclean—wrote about this very problem in Ireland:

> If you remove the English army tomorrow and hoist the green flag over Dublin Castle, unless you set about the organisation of the socialist republic, your efforts would be in vain—the capitalist class would still rule you.[3]

Maclean, one of the few on the British left to defend the Dublin Easter Rising in 1916, shared Connolly's view.

The SNP's solution is simple. There will be no change in the system of government and no real change in the corrupt society of which the present system of government is an integral part. Instead, says the SNP, as soon as we have our independent parliament in Edinburgh, its doors will open to a bright new future. It's like saying Coca Cola rots your teeth when bottled in London, but site the bottling plant at the foot of Edinburgh's Royal Mile and Coca Cola will be good for you.

Maclean's legacy

Britain has always been an imperialist state, but from the founding of the Friends of the People Society in 1792 the great majority of radicals, trade unionists and socialists in Scotland—with the exception of Thomas Muir in the 1790s and Maclean in the 1920s—opposed independence and assumed that democracy, and later socialism, could only be achieved on an all-British basis. They were right to do so at the time and Maclean was tactically wrong in calling for independence, even though he approached the question as an anti-imperialist and from a revolutionary socialist standpoint. Maclean was still highly regarded among the Scottish working class, as was shown by the thousands who lined

the streets for his funeral. But sadly, his Scottish Workers'
Republican Party, founded in the last year of his life, numbered its membership in the dozens and its electoral support
in mere hundreds.

Today the limits of devolution, the world recession and
the continued drive to war have changed the context in
which we operate. The British state has already begun to
fragment and to call for its break-up on an anti-war basis,
in a situation where the majority opposed the wars in Iraq,
Afghanistan and now Syria, means Scottish independence
can and should be supported for anti-imperialist as opposed
to nationalist ends—the position Maclean advocated after
1920. In a recently published collection of essays on the
referendum, Neil Davidson posed the question, what is
independence for?

> What then is Scottish independence for? It opens up a space
> for struggle—a space that can be filled either by the contin-
> uation of neoliberalism or by the beginning of an alternative
> but the only way to ensure that a Scottish successor state
> is not as committed to the capitalist agenda as the British
> one is to build self-confidence and solidarity in unions and
> working class communities now. And by emphasising the
> possibility of change now, the socialist elements in the yes
> campaign can make a link with those workers who are cur-
> rently opposed or unsure about independence. There are no
> guarantees and certainly no possibility of socialism being
> established within the boundaries of a Scottish state: but
> independence can be part of a process, which by weakening
> the neoliberal, imperialist state in Britain, can potentially
> bring the necessarily international basis of socialism closer.[4]

An independent Scotland would not be a socialist
Scotland. There is nothing intrinsically beneficial about
Scottish independence. To think otherwise is to encourage
the myth that the Scots are more left wing than the English

and that there can be a Scottish parliamentary road to socialism—a notion that John Maclean ridiculed. Workers in Scotland, Wales, England, Ireland and beyond will still need unity in struggle against those who rule us. But the break-up of the UK would be a small victory for the world working class and, as John Maclean argued 90 years ago, that is something to fight for.

I

Maclean's significance

The explosion of working class revolt during the First World War produced one of Britain's finest socialist leaders. In 1914 John Maclean broke with the leadership of his own party to become the most consistent opponent of British imperialism and the most prominent figure in the anti-war movement.

Maclean was a school teacher who became a leading figure on "Red Clydeside" at a time when the whole of Europe was in revolt. He was involved with the Clyde Workers' Committee (CWC)—a rank and file revolt against the dismantling of trade union defences during wartime. Yet he refused to subordinate socialist politics to trade unionism. As an international socialist, he criticised the leading shop stewards of the CWC when they failed to campaign inside the factories for strike action to stop the war.

Not only did he oppose the war, but he also campaigned against its immediate effect on the working class. He held regular anti-war meetings at the factory gates and outside army recruitment offices; he was involved in campaigns against rising food prices; and he played a leading role in the successful rents campaign of 1915, when a mass rent strike, allied to the threat of industrial action in the shipyards and munitions factories, forced the government to halt rent rises for the duration of the war.

Maclean became the outstanding British Marxist of his day. A consistent supporter of Irish independence, he was one of the very few figures on the British left to defend the 1916 Easter Rising against British colonial rule. He campaigned to connect socialist theory with the everyday experience of working people—organising regular classes on Marxist economics in the industrial towns and mining areas across central Scotland. At the height of the war his weekly class in Glasgow attracted 500 workers.

British Bolshevik

Maclean was an enthusiastic supporter of the 1917 Russian Revolution and was proud to call himself a Bolshevik. He spoke at mass rallies throughout Britain, urging workers to follow the example of Russia and turn the imperialist war into a socialist revolution. All of this brought him to the attention of the British government. Lloyd George's war cabinet saw him as a dangerous revolutionary, and Maclean was imprisoned on five separate occasions. Twice he was condemned to lengthy terms of penal servitude by the British state for sedition—and twice he was released through mass protest.

Lenin regarded Maclean as Britain's outstanding revolutionary leader. He was elected honorary president of the workers' government of Russia alongside Lenin and Trotsky, and appointed official soviet consul in Glasgow.

The First World War was ended by the revolt of the European working class. The victory of the soviets in Russia was followed by revolutions in Germany and Hungary. In the cities of northern Italy workers occupied their factories. In Ireland the guerrilla war was gathering momentum. These events resonated in Britain where, after four years of war, mass disaffection was escalating. In the first few months of 1919 the government was rocked by a wave of mass strikes and mutinies in the army, navy and police. Maclean argued that Britain, too, was "moving in the rapids of revolution".

Turning point

But the trade union leaders had no stomach for an all-out confrontation with the state. They preferred to sabotage the struggle and to allow the government to ride out the storm. Unlike Russia there was no mass revolutionary party to unite the working class. The failure of the German Revolution was a turning point. Its leader, Rosa Luxemburg, was murdered and the workers' state in Russia was left isolated. By the end of 1920 it was becoming clear that the tide of European revolution was receding.

In Britain the post-war recession brought with it a vicious employers' offensive. Workplace organisation was smashed and working class confidence diminished. In these changed circumstances Maclean's base crumbled and he looked for ways to overcome the retreat.

With the encouragement of Lenin and the Communist International, the Communist Party of Great Britain was belatedly formed over 1920-21. The Bolsheviks regarded Maclean as the authentic voice of the British revolution, yet he refused to join the new party because he had major political differences with those who would lead it. It was a serious error, which only increased his isolation.

He remained a convinced revolutionary and supporter of Lenin and the Communist International. But as an isolated individual he was unable to influence events. Towards the end of 1920 he began calling for a Scottish Workers' Republic; it was a gesture of opposition to the British Empire at a time when Ireland was becoming ungovernable. It was a miscalculation on Maclean's part but in keeping with his internationalism. Like the leaders of the Communist International, he regarded British imperialism as the biggest obstacle to world revolution.

He was only 44 years of age when he died from poverty and physical exhaustion in November 1923. His death was hastened by the hunger strikes, forced feeding and harsh treatment he endured in prison. 10,000 workers lined the streets of Glasgow for his funeral, but sadly, this courageous fighter left nothing behind in the way of a solid political organisation. Like other great revolutionaries of the period, Maclean never fully grasped the significance of the Bolshevik Party, even after the October Revolution in 1917.

This meant that for a long time after his death his contribution was ignored by orthodox historians and his legacy distorted by the reformist and Stalinist politicians who came to dominate the working class movement after his death.

Maclean and nationalism

In the recent past there has been a welcome revival of interest in John Maclean and a reassessment of his life and times by labour historians. While there is certainly a new audience for Maclean, there is also continuing controversy and debate about what he stood for.

In her otherwise inspiring biography, published in 1973, his daughter Nan Milton argued that he refused to join the Communist Party because he was already convinced of the need for Scottish independence and a separate Scottish Communist Party. The Scottish nationalists have taken this opportunity to claim him for their tradition. Short on heroes of their own and keen to present a radical alternative to Labour, they portray him as a left wing Scottish patriot.

The notion that Maclean was motivated by nationalism extends beyond the ranks of the SNP. The Scottish Trades Union Congress (STUC), the Labour Party and many on the Scottish left reject the idea of the working class as the agent of social change. They look instead to a devolved Scottish parliament to defend the Scottish economy and Scottish jobs. It is claimed that Maclean advocated such an approach towards the end of his life, but this misrepresents everything he stood for.

Revolution

In May 1921, on trial under the Emergency Regulations Acts, Maclean was asked by the state prosecutor what he had meant by the term "revolution". Maclean held out both of his hands, one above the other and said, "They represent the two classes in society; the top being the capitalist class." Then he reversed his hands and said, "That is revolution." The prosecutor was clearly alarmed and asked, "You want workers to seize other people's capital?" Maclean replied sharply, "The workers will seize the world".[5]

John Maclean was undoubtedly Britain's greatest revolutionary leader. The growing crisis of capitalism means that his ideas are just as relevant today.

2

Britain and the age of empire

John Maclean was born in 1879 and began his political activity at the turn of the century. It was the age of empire and Britain led the field in imperial expansion. British investment in foreign and colonial stock quadrupled between 1883 and 1889, and its exports increasingly went to the less developed world.

Britain had been the world's first industrial power, but where it led others followed. Virtually the whole of the globe was already carved up between the major capitalist powers—less than a dozen ruling classes in ruthless competition with each other. Between 1870 and 1900 the whole of sub-Saharan Africa was partitioned between seven European powers.

By the turn of the century Britain's imperial advantage was being rapidly eroded by the greater efficiency of German and American capital. But the United Kingdom of Great Britain and Ireland was still the wealthiest and most powerful state in the world—as both its leading industrial producer and its foremost financial centre. Britain's merchants dominated global shipping lanes, and its shipyards supplied 90 percent of the world's ships. The British ruling class had amassed the largest empire in world history, covering a quarter of humanity, and it still possessed the most powerful military machine.

Imperialism came at the expense of the exploited workers and peasants of the colonial world; but it was also paid for by the workers in the developed capitalist countries. In Britain real wages rose irregularly until 1895; from 1896 until 1900 wages remained static and thereafter they began to fall. Between 1900 and 1913 real wages declined by 10 percent.

The growth in poverty was no accident. Amid spectacular wealth the great majority of the British population experienced grim living conditions and brutal exploitation. Within a few years this obscene contradiction would explode in the Great Unrest—a prolonged period of mass working class revolt of unprecedented scale and ferocity, lasting from 1910 until 1914. This tidal wave of struggle swept mainland Britain and colonial Ireland, only to be abruptly ended by the onset of the war.

Scottish capital and the empire
There is a view that Scotland suffered national oppression as a result of the Act of Union in 1707, but there is no evidence to support it. The Scottish ruling class helped pioneer the British Empire and Scotland's capitalists profited tremendously, playing a role which was greater, comparative to their size, than England's. Throughout the Victorian age Scotland surpassed the other nations of the United Kingdom in its overseas investments.

The contrast with Ireland could not have been greater. Dominated and exploited by England and, later, Britain, Ireland's economy was deliberately stunted and the native Irish bourgeoisie never allowed to fully develop. Theobold Wolfe Tone, the Protestant lawyer who led the revolt of the United Irishmen in 1798, wrote, "England checks our rising commerce at every turn."

As a direct result of this oppression the Irish population fell by 3 million in the late 1840s. Not only did Scottish troops help to police this genocide, but Scottish capital played a key role in developing Ireland's one area of industrial development—the hinterland around Belfast.

Scotland was different from Ireland: far from being oppressed, Scotland benefited from the Act of Union. The Scottish ruling class became partners with England and the beneficiaries of industrial expansion and imperialism.

Glasgow's merchants benefited from slavery, and from the early industrial revolution onwards Scotland was pre-eminent in major export trades.

On Clydeside one wave of manufacturing followed another. Success in tobacco and cotton was supplemented by heavy industry and coal. The Clyde alone produced 70 percent of all iron tonnage launched in Britain between 1850 and 1870.

In 1879, the year John Maclean was born, the first steel-hulled ship was launched on the Clyde. By 1885, when steel was replacing iron, Clydeside produced 42 percent of all Siemens steel. Within a few years Clydeside accounted for 50 percent of the world's annual tonnage of shipping and became the biggest exporter of steam locomotives in the world.

By the start of the 20th century the Clyde Valley had become a centre of coalmining, shipbuilding, steel production and engineering. It contained Britain's biggest concentration of heavy industry and was one of the greatest centres of capital accumulation in the world. Its giant firms, and the Scottish dynasties which ran them, were tied in to the indigenous Scottish banking system, while at the same time they enjoyed privileged access to the British state.

Such a massive scale of production and investment demanded an enormous supply of labour, and while Scotland's industrialists and financiers grew fabulously wealthy, the masses who created this wealth suffered terribly at their hands. Throughout the 19th century men, women and children were driven in the tens of thousands from the Scottish Highlands and from rural Ireland by land clearances and famine. Thousands stopped off in the port of Glasgow on their way to the US and Canada—but thousands more stayed to work in the industrial hell that disfigured the Clyde Valley.

3

Becoming a socialist

John Maclean's parents, Daniel Maclean and Anne MacPhee, had both been child victims of the Highland Clearances. They had been driven with their parents from their crofts—his father from the Isle of Mull, his mother from Corpach near Fort William. John was born in Pollokshaws, Glasgow, in 1879, the sixth of seven children, only four of whom survived. When John was eight years old his father died from silicosis, an occupational lung disease caused by inhalation of dust, and his mother had to bring up the children on her own.

Despite intense poverty, John stayed on at school, becoming a pupil teacher when he was 17. In 1900 he qualified as a primary school teacher and was employed by the Govan School Board. Attending classes in his spare time at Glasgow University, he studied political economy and became absorbed by Marx's *Capital*. Marx's harrowing description of the Sutherland clearances must have sharpened his sense of class injustice, and along with his growing attachment to the ideas of socialism and Marxist economics, this led him towards political activism and organisation.

The Labour Representation Committee, the forerunner of the British Labour Party, had just been formed in 1900. It was unique among the parties of the European labour movement in its frank rejection of socialism. The driving force behind it, Keir Hardie's Independent Labour Party, was prepared to compromise on socialist ideals for electoral gain and the support of the trade union leaders. Maclean looked elsewhere.

In 1902 he joined the Glasgow branch of the Social Democratic Federation (SDF)—the first British Marxist organisation. This drew Maclean into the socialist movement, where he rapidly became a talented propagandist. But the SDF and its successor, the British Socialist Party (BSP), espoused a method and outlook that he would eventually break with. To understand how this shaped his political development we need to briefly examine European social democracy in the years before he joined. "Social democracy" in Maclean's time had a different meaning from its present one. In its pre-1914 sense, it meant the international socialist perspectives of the Second International, drawing on the ideas of Marx and Engels.

The Second International and the SDF

Britain's long period of industrial supremacy, the elitism of its existing craft unions, and their subordination to the Liberal Party retarded the development of an independent workers' movement until the start of the 20th century. This presented real difficulties for Marx's followers in Britain. The SDF was formed in 1884. It claimed allegiance to Marxism—specifically the Marxism of European social democracy, whose proponents founded the Second International in 1889 to link together socialist organisations throughout the world.

European social democracy was based on mass workers' parties, the German Social Democratic Party being the biggest and most influential. But the socialist parties that constituted the Second International shared a serious political weakness: in certain key respects their Marxism contradicted the revolutionary ideas that Marx had developed. The writings of Marx and Engels were meant to be a guide to action, stressing the unity of theory and practice and the role of conscious human activity. However, Second International Marxism, as developed by its leading theoretician, Karl Kautsky, led to different conclusions.

Kautsky argued that it was inevitable that capitalism would collapse and socialism would follow. This mechanical approach to history was a departure from Marx and implied that socialist parties had a relatively passive role to play— their primary functions being to educate their members, to produce socialist propaganda and to contest elections. The hallmark of the Second International was parliamentarianism, a significant break from the conclusion reached by Marx after the defeat of the Paris Commune in 1871 that the state must be forcefully overthrown.

In the British case the shortcomings of Second International Marxism were magnified by the SDF. It was small and isolated from the working class like no other party in Europe, and while it managed to attract a significant number of workers to its public meetings and rallies, it responded to a difficult situation in a sectarian manner. In a country where reformist politics and gradualism were deeply rooted in the workers' movement, the SDF reflected rather than overcame the division between politics and economics.

Cut off from immediate influence within the organised working class, the early British Marxists of the SDF adopted a purely propagandist role—explaining the economic laws of capitalism and preparing workers for the inevitable victory of socialism. The SDF was further hampered by the peculiarities of its creator, H M Hyndman—a Tory stockbroker who claimed his outlook had changed after reading Marx's *Capital*.

Unfortunately he never abandoned his British chauvinism or his haughty contempt for ordinary workers. When Hyndman plagiarised Marx's *Capital* for his own book, *England For All*, the reason he gave for failing to acknowledge his debt to Marx was that British workers would not accept the ideas if they knew that they came from a foreigner. Needless to say, Marx and Engels had little time for either Hyndman or his organisation.

Formed at a time when trade unionism and the industrial struggle were at a low level, the SDF was too conservative to rise to the challenge when the working class moved into action. Although individual Marxists in the SDF played a key role in the mass strikes of the "New Unionism" in 1889, Hyndman and his friends opposed such intervention. As a party, the SDF turned its back on the struggle, dismissing strike action as futile. Hyndman claimed that trade unions were the bulwark of capitalism and deplored the great London dock strike as "a lowering of the flag, a departure from active propaganda and a waste of energy".

The leadership of the SDF regarded the dissemination of Marxist propaganda as its real purpose, while trade unionism and strikes were seen as useless diversions. Engels correctly summed up the SDF as: "Reducing the Marxist theory of development to a rigid orthodoxy, which workers are not to reach by their own class consciousness, but which, like an article of faith, is to be forced down their throats at once and without development".[6]

The Socialist Labour Party and syndicalism

With the rise of industrial struggle at the beginning of the century, some SDF members became increasingly critical of the leadership. In 1903 there was a split, which led to the formation of the Socialist Labour Party (SLP). Based mainly in Scotland, the breakaway effectively halved the SDF's already tiny Scottish membership.

The SLP attached great importance to the struggle at the point of production. For the first time in Britain a small Marxist group tried to connect revolutionary politics with the workplace. Following the ideas of the American socialist Daniel De Leon, a founding member of the Industrial Workers of the World, and the Irish revolutionary James Connolly, the SLP advocated the formation of industrial unions to replace the existing craft organisations.

The SLP argued there should be one union for each industry, and that these industrial unions would serve both as a means of fighting capitalism in the here and now and as the basis of the future socialist society. But like the SDF, the SLP had major handicaps: it emphasised the need for the reorganisation of the unions at the expense of socialist politics and the building of a workers' political party.

Syndicalism had become very popular among working class militants, as it represented a reaction against the obvious shortcomings of parliamentary politics and conciliatory trade unionism. But within the broader stream of syndicalism the SLP acted like a small sect—counterposing the idea of industrial unions to the existing unions and refusing to relate to rank and file movements not under its control. Its sectarianism eventually forced James Connolly into breaking with it. Not surprisingly, it never comprised more than a few hundred members, most of them based in Glasgow.

Despite its weaknesses, the SLP would go on to play an important role during the First World War, when its significance was quite out of proportion to its actual size.

It became the main focus of political activity within the shop stewards' movement in engineering—proof that even a handful of organised socialists can make a difference to what happens in the world around them. But as an organisation the SLP was a mirror image of the SDF. J T Murphy, an engineering steward at the giant Vickers munitions plant in Sheffield, became a leading member of the SLP. In his book, *Preparing for Power*, he recalls that, "None of us saw a political party as anything other than a propaganda body for the spread of socialist ideas".[7]

Meanwhile, Hyndman's SDF amalgamated with other groups, becoming first the Social Democratic Party (SDP) in 1908, then the British Socialist Party (BSP) in 1911. Unfortunately it never managed to change its approach. Like its rival the SLP, it continued to operate as a propaganda body, unable to grow despite the biggest explosion of working class struggle that Britain had yet seen. Despite calls from among its better members to carry out systematic work inside the unions, and despite the activity of individuals like John Maclean, it confined itself to abstract political debates and continued to ignore industrial struggle.

This didn't mean that there were no leading trade union militants in the SDF/BSP, and in fact a significant industrial unionist faction remained in the BSP right through the pre-war years, Willie Gallacher being the most prominent example. But the industrial struggle was never taken seriously and the BSP remained a marginal presence in the working class movement.

The not-so-red Clyde

When John Maclean joined the SDF, though still in his early twenties, he soon found a role in the organisation. In 1903 he established himself as a prominent local speaker. This was partly due to his energy and dedication but it was also down to necessity, as at that point the SDF had very few members in Scotland.

Some socialists insist Scotland was and is naturally more radical and left wing than England, and that John Maclean and the Red Clyde are explained by the fact that Scotland was a hotbed of socialism. This same argument is often used to champion independence today. It is a myth.

At the turn of the century Scotland was one of the most advanced capitalist countries in the world, yet independent working class trade union and political organisation was still relatively narrow and undeveloped. When Maclean joined the SDF its Scottish membership numbered less than 200, and the Marxist movement was much smaller and weaker than its counterpart in England. This was no accident—it was a reflection of the relative backwardness of the Scottish working class movement at the time.

John Maclean

When the great wave of New Unionism began in 1889, Clydeside largely missed out. The growth of union membership among the unskilled had less impact on Glasgow than on other industrial centres in Britain. As a result, trade union membership remained confined to a relatively small number of skilled craft workers. So weak and ineffectual was trade unionism in Scotland when Maclean joined the SDF, that in 1903 he wrote a letter to *The Scottish Co-operator* pointing out the irrelevance of "that clumsy weapon, the strike". For the next few years he devoted more of his time and energy to the co-operative movement than he did to the unions.

It was only after visiting Belfast during the great dock strike of 1907 that he became really enthusiastic about the impact that trade union activity could have on working class political consciousness. This changed his outlook and helped him to break from the inherent sectarianism of his own organisation. Clydeside was affected by the Great Unrest in the years leading up to the war, but it was not in the vanguard of the movement which, in other parts of Britain, reached insurrectionary proportions. In 1911, while on a speaking tour of South Wales in support of the Cambrian miners' strike, Maclean wrote of being ashamed to receive complaints from Welsh strike leaders about the lack of solidarity from Scottish miners.

Scotland also lagged behind politically. Until the end of the First World War it was dominated by the Liberals. In Keir Hardie's first attempt to stand as a Labour candidate in mid-Lanark, where he was born, he polled a derisory 600 votes. To win a parliamentary seat he had to contest West Ham in the heart of London's docklands. In the 1910 general election, the last before the outbreak of war, Labour's percentage share of the vote in Scotland was half its overall percentage share in Britain. Scotland returned three Labour MPs compared to 42 MPs for Britain as a whole. Keir

Hardie's 1913 pamphlet, *All about the ILP* (Independent Labour Party), does not mention Scotland once.

The turning point came with the war, when Clydeside became the key centre of arms manufacturing. It was the war economy and its impact on the skilled metal workers that made the Clyde a focal point of labour unrest, trade union militancy and socialist agitation.

But in this sense the Clyde was not unique. Across Europe all the big centres of the metal industry were transformed and radicalised by the war. The expansion of mass production undermined the position of skilled craftsmen, creating new layers of unskilled and semi-skilled workers drawn from the countryside and among women.

Turin, Berlin and Petrograd all saw the rise of revolutionary movements whose core was the skilled metal workers. The Clyde was part of a wider European movement that involved the other British engineering centres of Sheffield, Coventry, Manchester, Tyneside, Barrow and Belfast.

4

A model social democrat

If the war was the turning point for Clydeside, it was also the turning point for Maclean; it marked his break with the Second International and led to a dramatic change in his political status which brought him to international attention.

When he joined the SDF in 1902 the prospects of a revolution in Britain seemed remote. Clydeside was firmly in the grip of Liberalism and regarded as hostile territory by reformists, let alone Marxists. But in the space of 13 years everything was turned upside down.

After Maclean's death his role in this dramatic period was almost erased from history. In the attempt to set the record straight some well-meaning biographers have assumed or implied that, from his earliest days in the SDF, he was the most prominent and consistent opponent of Hyndman and the right wing leadership. Unfortunately this is not true, and to pretend otherwise only obscures Maclean's real development as a revolutionary socialist.

From 1917 he was a representative of Bolshevism in Britain. But by then he had been forced to reject a great deal of what he had adopted and absorbed in his early years in the socialist movement. When, in 1903, half the Scottish membership of the SDF left out of disgust with Hyndman to form the SLP, Maclean had already been a member of the SDF for about a year. He chose to remain in the SDF and for the next eight years his political line was largely consistent with Hyndman's.

Recent research confirms this. The historians Ripley and McHugh have argued that:

Had he died in 1910, Maclean would be remembered, if at all, as a loyal Scottish Hyndmanite. Up to this point there is little in Maclean's public statements to suggest his political line is other than consistent with the position of the social democratic "old guard" and especially Hyndman and Quelch, with whom he maintained good personal relations... This is not to say Maclean was a mere cipher for Hyndman or Quelch but to underline the fact that he was very much a Marxist in the orthodox social democratic mould.[8]

From 1903 until 1910 he did not oppose Hyndman on any significant matter. When he finally did in 1911, he stayed inside the BSP, as it was then called, and remained a model social democrat in the tradition of the Second international until 1914. Harry McShane, a lifelong Marxist revolutionary and one of Maclean's closest associates, recalls the significance of this:

Like most Marxists before 1914, John Maclean was an admirer of the German Social Democratic Party, then the largest socialist party in the world and making great electoral conquests. Apart from the first volume of *Capital*, very few of Marx's writings were available in English but the gap seemed to be almost filled by the popular works of Karl Kautsky, the German socialist leader. The German socialists seemed to set the pattern in both theory and practice.[9]

John Maclean was commonly described as a principled, intransigent Marxist. But he was also willing to learn and able to adapt quickly to events around him. When he started coming to terms with the momentous events developing in Britain and internationally, he began to reject some of his earlier assumptions.

In 1908 a young Russian political prisoner of the defeated 1905 Revolution escaped from Siberia and arrived in the port of Leith. He was sent to John Maclean, who was well known in the socialist movement for his generosity and hospitality. The young man was Peter Petroff and he would go on to play a significant role in Maclean's life. After leaving Glasgow, Petroff went to London, joined the SDF and rose to prominence in its left wing. He would later become an important ally, sharing Maclean's revolutionary attitude to the war. Like Maclean, Petroff would also spend time in a British jail for his internationalism, and in 1918 the British government deported him back to Russia.

In 1909 Maclean married Agnes Wood, whom he'd first met during one of his summer speaking tours in 1906. They had two daughters—Jean, born in 1911, and Nan, in 1913. Maclean at this time continued to work as a school teacher and to maintain his commitment to the SDF.

The experience of struggle

The most significant development in Maclean's politics during this period concerned the rising tide of industrial militancy. As we have already seen, the SDF was dismissive of trade unions and working class agency. When the scale of class struggle began to escalate from around 1907, the SDF proved incapable of relating to it; not so Maclean.

Initially, in keeping with orthodox social democracy, he was pessimistic about the role of unions and the value of strikes. Until 1907 his view was jaundiced by his experiences on Clydeside. It was an area where unionisation had made no real impact on the unskilled and remained narrowly focused on organising the relatively skilled workers of the engineering, shipbuilding and mining industries. This led him to stress the limitations of strikes and trade union activity, which he saw as necessary but essentially defensive in character. However, in 1907 his involvement in the great Belfast dock strike resulted in a dramatic change in attitude.

This was a strike by the poorest workers in Belfast. For the first time unskilled protestant and Catholic labourers fought side by side against the Unionist bosses and the forces of the state.

Battleships were sent to Belfast Lough, troops attacked the strikers—killing three—and cavalry were used to put down riots. The burden of protecting scab labour provoked a police mutiny and the entire city was thrown into chaos.

Maclean had been invited to Ireland by James Larkin, a militant union organiser who led the strike. When Maclean arrived in Belfast he was energised by the dramatic events and spoke at mass rallies in support of the strikers. His diary of the visit was printed in the SDF's newspaper, *Justice*:

> Addressed strikers at night...an audience of thousands. Labourers are mad keen to join the trade union...all Irish towns are the same. Had three monster meetings...about 10,000 present, though some estimated 15,000. Had a meeting of 1,000 on Monday night.[10]

Maclean left Belfast exhilarated. For the first time he had witnessed the politicising effect of a major industrial struggle on masses of workers and he recorded how this changed his outlook:

> Strikes reveal the underlying reality of capitalism and the class war in ways that are more effective than all the theory we might fire at our benighted class from now till doomsday... Fighting leads to new facts, thus to our new theory, thence to revolution.[11]

From then on he would be quick to recognise the revolutionary potential of trade union militancy whenever it raised its head: the Great Unrest in 1909, strikes in Paisley involving young women mill workers, the Dublin Lockout of 1913, the anti-dilution strikes in the Clydeside munitions plants during wartime, and the mass strikes at the end of the war.

The Great Unrest

From 1910 to 1914 Britain was convulsed by the Great Unrest, when a series of ferocious struggles led by rank and file militants brought masses of workers into conflict with their employers, the state and the trade union bureaucracy. It was a period of unprecedented militancy, involving all-out battles in transport and mining, spontaneous rank and file strikes by the low paid and the unorganised, mass strikes by women textile workers, challenges by skilled workers to the right of managers to operate machinery as they saw fit, strikes against the employment of non-union labour, and strikes like the great Dublin Lockout, which won solidarity with workers in Britain.

Throughout this period many new, young working class militants were attracted to the ideas of industrial unionism and syndicalism. Clydeside was by no means the centre of this movement, but it was affected by it. Significantly, the growing number of industrial disputes was not restricted to the traditional sectors of coalmining, shipbuilding and engineering. Women and unskilled men reacted against the new production methods associated with an extreme division of labour based on assembly line production.

An example was the famous Singers Sewing Machine strike at Clydebank in 1911. Singers, an American company, had built a new plant that employed 12,000 workers, about a quarter of whom were women. The factory was at the forefront of technological and managerial innovation. Virtually all the workforce was unskilled and production was based on assembly lines. The strike started when a handful of women struck against a speed-up and within days the entire factory was on strike. The struggle was led by a group of young SLP members around Tom Bell. The strike was eventually defeated, partly due to tactical errors. Although all the SLP activists involved were penalised, they were subsequently dispersed around the Clydeside engineering plants and played a key role in the shop stewards' movement in 1915.

Maclean analysed the strike and its lessons in the BSP newspaper, *Justice*. He saw it as the shape of things to come, pointing out that as deskilling became more prevalent, unions would have to amalgamate across sector and gender and to organise workers they had previously ignored. He was later proved right when, during the war, dilution—the introduction of unskilled men and women into work previously done by skilled engineers—became paramount.

More and more he was drawn towards struggle. His involvement in the massive coal strikes of 1911 and 1912 took him to the Rhondda Valley, where he was involved in a bitter strike between the South Wales miners and the Cambrian Coal Company. This dispute was a rank and file revolt, led by younger activists who had been influenced by the ideas of syndicalism.

Instead of castigating the SLP members who led the Singers strike or the young syndicalists of the Rhondda, Maclean was now keen to relate to them politically. He distinguished between correctly arguing that strikes raise class consciousness and falling into the trap of syndicalism. The existing revolutionary organisations had reinforced the division between politics and economics. On the one hand, the SDF openly scorned strikes as a diversion from political propaganda, while on the other hand the SLP insisted that political organisation was secondary to industrial organisation.

The approach that Maclean now adopted marked a breakthrough. He would continue to argue the primacy of politics over sectional struggle, but he broke from orthodox social democracy's pessimistic attitude towards strikes and the unions. In this respect Maclean was unusual, if not unique, among the "orthodox" Marxists in Britain. Social democracy was really about socialism through parliament. Maclean's experience of workers' struggles led him to challenge that approach. His change of attitude helps explain why he rose to such prominence during the anti-war struggles on the Clyde, and why he advocated workers' power and later moved towards Bolshevism in 1917. At one of his later trials he would tell the court, "I argued that the workers should not confine themselves to industrial action but should take political action as well. Neither political nor industrial action would do separately."

Breaking from Hyndman

At the end of 1910 Hyndman supported calls for a bigger navy and a massive increase in the British defence budget. He shared the view of leading Liberal and Conservative politicians that Germany's programme of naval expansion was a threat to British interests and that a "big navy" was the best way of combating that threat. Jingoism was being stirred up by the establishment and by rabid editorials in the national press, but for Britain's most prominent Marxist to endorse such militarism and side with the British ruling class was a major blow to those social democrats who took internationalism seriously.

The SDF (after 1911 the British Socialist Party) was deeply divided. Leading members supported Hyndman, but many branches opposed him. It is widely assumed that Maclean was one of the leaders of the anti-Hyndman campaign. Yet for most of the time between 1910 and 1914 he did not play a prominent role in this struggle.

Maclean was clearly committed to the internationalist position and he won his own Pollokshaws branch of the party to an anti-Hyndman stance in 1910, as seen in his declaration that:

> This branch recognises the international solidarity of the working class and deprecates Comrade Hyndman's agitation for a big navy as tending to break down rather than build up the essential unity of the working class.[12]

In this motion Maclean's tone is neither sharp nor polemical. While he opposed the right wing he did not confront them head-on until 1913. He was a regular Scottish contributor to the BSP newspaper *Justice* but his articles between 1911 and 1913 do not reflect the struggle inside the organisation. The historian Walter Kendall, who was generally sympathetic towards Maclean, noted that "Maclean's role in the internal struggles of the BSP before the war is rather limited".[13]

There are two reasons for this. First, Maclean's faith in social democracy meant that he regarded Hyndman's position as an aberration. Like Lenin, he expected the anti-war position of the German SPD to be carried in the event of war. With hindsight, Maclean might appear naive, but at the time he was in very good company. Lenin, the most sober of revolutionaries, was an admirer of German social democracy up until 1914. Rosa Luxemburg, "the greatest brain in the Marxist movement", was a member of the German party and she was stunned when the SPD parliamentary group voted to support the war effort.

The second reason for Maclean's failure to lead the fight stemmed from his conception of the socialist party and the role of its members. The SDF had always operated as a socialist sect and as a result it missed out on the mass strikes of the New Unionism and the Great Unrest. It was a loose federalist body in which differences were tolerated but never resolved, an organisation where members—especially the old guard—were rarely held to account and could go their own way. It was more like a debating society than a serious socialist party, whose members argue out a position and then fight in unison to win it in the outside world.

Unfortunately, Maclean accepted this. While he was fully committed to the idea of a Marxist political organisation, he knew of no alternative to the social democratic model then on offer. He was unwilling to leave the party, or to force a split as Lenin had already done in Russia. At this time, at any rate, he had no knowledge of Lenin. For Maclean, personal integrity was a substitute for a lack of party discipline and accountability.

The turning point

In 1913, as his differences with the leadership grew, Maclean began to take a more prominent role in the opposition to Hyndman. In Easter 1914 he attended the BSP national conference and, along with his friend Peter Petroff, he made an open challenge to the right wing leadership. Maclean wanted the party's newspaper *Justice* removed from Hyndman's control, and for the conference to mandate all BSP election candidates to stand on the programme laid down by the membership. The fact that he was defeated and could not win a majority of conference delegates on such basic issues of party democracy proved that the BSP was utterly incapable of providing leadership in the struggles that lay ahead. Maclean was disenchanted, but continued to pursue his own course within the party. Although he remained a member, his activities were increasingly undertaken on his own initiative, and not in any sense under the direction of the BSP leadership.

By 1914 John Maclean had been an active socialist for over a decade. He had established his reputation as a gifted orator through his regular Marxist classes and his summer speaking tours of the major Scottish towns. But despite his internationalist outlook, his political activity had been restricted geographically. Outside of the small provincial milieu of Scottish socialists and trade union activists, he was relatively unknown. But the outbreak of war and Maclean's opposition to it would transform him from a figure of relative obscurity into a socialist of international renown.

5

The outbreak of war

On 4 August 1914 the long predicted war between the imperialist powers broke out. It was a war for colonies, for spheres of influence, for markets. It was, in short, a war for profits. And it shattered the international socialist movement. The leaders of the major social democratic parties abandoned the principles of Marxism and internationalism and capitulated to their own governments.

Four years previously, at the International Socialist Congress in Copenhagen, these self-same leaders had passed a motion reaffirming that it was the duty of socialists to prevent the outbreak of war by all possible means:

> Should war nevertheless break out, their duty is to intervene to promptly bring it to an end and with all their energies to use the political and economic crisis created by the war to rouse the populace from its slumbers and to hasten the fall of capitalist domination.[14]

Instead, with the outbreak of war, they entered their various national governments to help the war effort. "It seems only yesterday", wrote Lenin in 1915:

> that Hyndman having turned to the defence of imperialism prior to the war, was looked upon by all decent socialists as an unbalanced crank and that nobody spoke of him otherwise than in a tone of disdain. Now the most eminent Social Democrat leaders of all the countries have sunk to Hyndman's position.[15]

Maclean in the minority

Britain in the years leading up to the war had seen a great wave of working class struggle from below. Between 1911 and 1914 trade union membership had doubled. The war acted as a sudden brake, so that the situation seemed to change abruptly.

The fact that it was fought between nations of enormous industrial capacity meant it was arguably the first industrial war, where all economic life was directed towards war production by the state. The government was forced to intervene directly in economic production. It introduced rationing and took over key firms. Crucially, it pushed through the Munitions Act of 1915 and the Defence of the Realm Act of 1914, draconian measures which suspended civil liberties, banned strikes, imposed compulsory arbitration and stopped workers from changing jobs.

The government whipped up a wave of jingoism. Labour party leaders contributed to the nationalist fervour and trade union leaders backed the war. They spoke at recruitment rallies and told trade unionists to forget about wage rises and pull together in the national interest. These appeals met with widespread success. Socialist and working class organisations were divided.

With the outbreak of war Hyndman and the executive leadership of the BSP urged its members to actively and enthusiastically support the war effort—including through the participation of party speakers on recruiting platforms. Hyndman argued that this position could be justified in Marxist terms as the defence of Belgium from the reactionary German state.

The majority of BSP members opposed this decision, and the London branches overwhelmingly rejected it. But a majority of the opposition were themselves conflicted, either adopting a pacifist approach, or arguing for "defencism"— whereby war could be supported in so far as it was a defence against German aggression, rather than for territorial advantage.

As far as Maclean was concerned none of these positions were tenable. Right from the start he argued that the war could not be supported on any terms. On the day war was declared he was on holiday with his family at Tarbert on the Firth of Clyde. He went round the town chalking the streets with anti-war and anti-government slogans. He came back to Glasgow and immediately organised an open air meeting on Glasgow Green, where he argued for a revolutionary anti-war position. Like Lenin, he saw the war as a struggle between the great powers for land and markets:

> Plunderers versus plunderers with the workers as pawns. It is our business as socialists to develop class patriotism, refusing to murder one another for a sordid world capitalism.[16]

He argued that if Germany was engaged in an expansionist policy then the German working class was its gravedigger. He insisted that a capitalist settlement of the war could only lead to further wars between the capitalist powers. Maclean's position stood out like a sore thumb.

Harry McShane was also prominent in the anti-war movement in Glasgow. At the time he was a member of the BSP and a young engineering shop steward in Weir's munitions plant—the cradle of the first shop stewards' movement. In his biography, *No Mean Fighter*, he explains the initial response of the left:

> Even though we didn't expect how terrible the war was going to be, we knew it was a political disaster. Our hopes for an international general strike to stop the war were unfounded. Every section of the Second International supported its own country's war effort. Only a few revolutionaries stood out—Lenin's Bolsheviks in Russia and Rosa Luxemburg and Karl Liebknecht in Germany... In Britain

the socialist movement was split over the war. Many socialists were also pacifists. In the ILP there was a good deal
of anti-war feeling but the leaders of the ILP took a very
weak stand and the national policy of the ILP was not clear.
In February 1915 Keir Hardie presided over a meeting in
London of socialists from the allied countries that actually
declared in favour of an allied victory.[17]

These comments are supported by the fact that Keir
Hardie told a meeting in his Merthyr constituency, "A
nation at war must be united—with the boom of enemy
guns within earshot the lads who have gone forth to fight
must not be disheartened by any discordant note at home".[18]
Like Keir Hardie, George Lansbury, editor of the *Daily
Herald*, was a well-known pacifist but after war broke out he
refused to print resolutions opposing it in the paper.

Collapse of the official left
McShane recalls that as the official left collapsed, Maclean
stood out firm against the war:

> Of the 17 ILP councillors in Glasgow, only two came
> out against the war—John Wheatley and John Taylor.
> Emmanuel Shinwell (ILP councillor and organiser for the
> British Seafarers' Union—and later Lord Shinwell) never
> committed himself at all. Hyndman and the leadership of
> the BSP were organising war propaganda and using *Justice*
> to put forward pro-war policies. In Glasgow we beat the
> pro-war faction of the BSP. A lot of the labour leaders were
> worse than Hyndman. Ben Tillet (leader of the Dockers'
> Union) toured the country telling how he had seen a greasy
> spot on a wall where a German had bashed a baby's brains
> out. He poured out atrocity stories against the Germans
> and became hateful, really damn well hateful. And there
> were others who did the same. Victor Grayson, who influ-
> enced me and thousands like me also went pro-war... John

Maclean held Sunday afternoon meetings at Nelson's Monument throughout the war. He also started them on Sunday evenings in Bath Street, outside the army recruiting centre. Although the ILP wasn't doing much about the war, their best elements were coming to our meetings—so were the SLPers, who openly opposed the war. John Maclean held the anti-war propaganda together.[19]

The movement that Maclean held together during the early months was, as yet, tiny. But it would soon have an opportunity to grow by relating to struggles around practical social and economic issues which arose from the capitalist nature of the war. Maclean, armed with a clear Marxist understanding of the conflict and committed to working class struggle and internationalism, would rise to the challenge.

6

War on two fronts

In the first months of the war strikes almost ceased. Between January and July of 1914 some 9 million days had been lost. But from August, when war was declared, to December of that year only a further 1 million days were lost. The employers and government felt confident that they could drive through radical changes in work practises and increase production.

Early in the war German industrial superiority became clear when tens of thousands of British soldiers were killed in the trenches for lack of weaponry. For British capitalism it was a life and death struggle, and war production became the ruling class's primary concern. In 1915 Liberal prime minister Herbert Asquith decided to form a national coalition with all the major parties, including the Labour Party. Lloyd George was put in charge of the war drive and responded by reorganising the munitions industry. The war in the trenches was accompanied by a domestic offensive against the working class to cut wages and increase exploitation.

In addition to the Defence of the Realm Act and the Munitions Act, the government signed a Treasury Agreement with most trade union leaderships in March 1915. These measures combined to deprive the working class of their right to negotiate and the right to strike, at a time when the ruling class was introducing dilution.

This practice of introducing unskilled labour on employers' terms was an immediate assault on the wages and conditions of skilled workers. But the threat was not confined to the duration of the war—it could permanently weaken traditional bargaining power and jeopardise jobs in the future.

There were more generalised attacks on the working class too. Prices had been rising from 1900, but with the war they rose much more steeply. According to official figures, in the first 12 months of the war food prices rose on average by 32 percent, and rents skyrocketed. Rationing was introduced in response to shortages, but there was no control over prices.

Industry started to boom and, as soldiers fell at the front and workers suffered at home, profits rose. Through their own experiences, ordinary people began to see that many employers were benefiting from the slaughter. The disparity between the wealth of the elites and the suffering of the masses fuelled discontent. In less than a year the initial euphoria had evaporated and class consciousness began to reassert itself. New struggles erupted, and out of them grew new forms of workers' organisation.

Glasgow: the first flashpoint

The first major industrial revolt of the war occurred in Glasgow, where a number of factors combined to produce a flashpoint. Skilled engineers were in an especially powerful position during the war. While most industries stagnated or declined, the metal industry, which produced the guns, shells, tanks, and ships, expanded rapidly.

Other workers could be intimidated with the threat of conscription, while engineers felt relatively safe, for they knew a skilled munitions worker was more useful to British capitalism in a factory than in a trench at the front. This gave the engineers who were under threat from dilution the leverage and confidence to confront the employers and the government.

As a key munitions area, Glasgow had a high proportion of skilled workers, and a large proportion of its workforce was organised. Glasgow also had a tradition of shop floor organisation. By 1914 both Beardmore's at Parkhead and Weir's of Cathcart had shop stewards committees, which was unusual at the time. This confidence and organisation served as a starting point for wartime militancy. But muscle and organisation don't automatically lead to action. Before the war the Clydeside engineers, due to their relative job security and high wages, were conservative and elitist in their outlook. But wartime conditions and the attempt to overhaul working practices combined to drive the skilled engineers into class struggle.

On Clydeside tensions and privations were particularly acute due to overcrowding. The massive increase in war production meant skilled labour was at a premium. Workers from across Britain flocked to Glasgow to work in munitions. This aggravated the appalling housing shortage in the city, where half the population lived in two-roomed houses and an eighth in single rooms. It also pushed up rents.

In Glasgow there was also the presence of a small but active grouping of anti-war socialists and syndicalists, influenced by John Maclean and rooted in key munitions plants. The SLP in particular had a number of young skilled workers in engineering. Willie Gallacher, a member of the BSP and convenor of the shop stewards at the Albion works, was a key participant. In his autobiography he recalled the importance of Maclean's factory gate meetings and his Marxist economic classes, which attracted hundreds of workers at a time:

> Maclean never dealt in abstract Marxism of the Kautsky variety. He applied his Marxist knowledge to the events around him and used all that was happening to show the truth of Marxism. He demonstrated in the clearest manner that the war was a war for trade and brought out into full relief the sinister robber forces behind it. He gave example after example of the financiers and the big employers pointing a gun at the head of the government, and demanding increased profits, and of other firms selling war materials to neutrals with the full knowledge that they were being resold to Germany... These examples were carried day after day into the factories.[20]

The first strike

The Glasgow engineers' pay claim provided the spark for the first strike of the war in February 1915. Sharp price rises and shortages affected skilled workers as well as the poor. In engineering there had been a national agreement, which had expired, and in Glasgow the local branches of the engineers' union, the ASE, demanded an increase of two pence on the hourly rate. But the government and the employers, who were making huge profits, were determined to drive down wages, attack conditions and destroy shop floor organisation.

The employers rejected the engineers' claim and the union officials refused to organise action to win it. They would have had to call strikes that sabotaged the war effort and there was never any chance of this. Meanwhile, Maclean and individuals from the SLP, the ILP and the BSP held factory gate meetings connecting the wage claim to the wider question of the war's relation to capitalism. Anger spilled over into strike action when 2,000 workers walked out at Weir's of Cathcart.

At the core of the strike were shop stewards elected from each section within the plant. Many of the old ASE stewards, whose only job had been to check union cards and collect dues, had been replaced by enthusiastic youngsters, influenced by socialist and syndicalist ideas. Within four days 10,000 workers from 26 different factories were out in support and demanding the two pence an hour. As Arthur McManus, a shop steward at Weir's and a member of the SLP, commented, "The one fact that struck home was the necessity of the workers doing for themselves what the officials were too cowardly to attempt".[21]

The bosses and the government did not use the law against the strikers. Then, as now, they knew their laws were ineffective in the face of mass defiance. Instead they employed divide and rule tactics. But, as the *Scottish Daily Record* reported:

Even when tempting offers have been made to sections of the strikers, the men have resolutely declined to divide their forces and all along they have contended that no one will start work until all have been satisfied.[22]

Solidarity was based on organisation via the Labour Withholding Committee, a strike committee linking stewards from different plants across the city. Opposed by the employers, the government and their own trade union leaders, the workers set up their own organisation, which later became the Clyde Workers' Committee. Willie Gallacher, who eventually became its chairman, explained: "Every morning mass meetings were held in the areas and the discussions and decisions of the previous day's committee meetings were reported".[23]

The men remained out for weeks, in defiance of the union officials. The strike committee eventually had to call a retreat and organised a united return to work to assert its own authority. Although they won only another penny an hour, a new kind of organisation had emerged. Far from being demoralised, the strike had strengthened the rank and file and fanned the flames of resistance. Soon that resistance would turn into political action against poor housing and rising rents on Clydeside.

Resistance also spread to the South Wales coalfield, a stronghold of trade union militancy in the pre-war period. In July 1915 200,000 Welsh miners, led by revolutionary syndicalists, struck for a wage increase. The strike was declared illegal under the Munitions Act, but such was the level of solidarity that the government was humiliated and forced to grant all of the miners' demands.

The struggle threatened to flare up again on Clydeside in the summer of 1915, when the government tried to enforce its anti-strike laws. In July a shop steward at Parkhead forge, the biggest munitions plant on the Clyde, was dismissed. He was brought to court, accused of "slacking and causing others to slack" and sentenced to three months in jail. Workers threatened a strike and eventually he was released and returned to work. A month later 17 shop stewards at Fairfield's shipyard in Govan were fined for leading a strike, and when three of the stewards accepted John Maclean's advice and refused to pay their fines, they were jailed. Maclean immediately led a campaign for their release and after a fortnight in prison they were freed because the government feared a strike across the Clyde. At Weir's a shop steward was charged with "molesting" a worker, merely for asking him for his union card. Two hundred of his workmates turned up at his court hearing to make it clear that no fine would be paid and that imprisonment would cause an immediate strike. The charges were dropped.

The Clyde Workers' Committee

On the back of such victories, the city-wide shop stewards' organisation was revived, and re-established as the Clyde Workers' Committee (CWC). Three hundred or so delegates met every weekend in Glasgow, the vast majority being stewards in engineering and the shipyards. Apart from the secretary James Messer and Davy Kirkwood, both of whom were in the ILP, all of its other leading members were revolutionaries belonging to the SLP or BSP.

John Maclean was not an elected member of the committee, but such was his standing that, along with his supporters Peter Petroff and James MacDougall, he was accepted as having an important contribution to make to the committee, and was allowed to attend its meetings and participate in its debates. Indeed it is doubtful that the leaders of the CWC would have taken the lead in industrial matters had it not been for Maclean's efforts to show that the war served only imperialist interests and should be opposed by the workers.

The CWC was not an alternative to the trade unions, nor was it set up in opposition to them. Its attitude to the trade union bureaucracy was succinctly expressed in the committee's first leaflet, produced in November 1915:

We will support the officials just so long as they rightly represent the workers, but we will act independently immediately they misrepresent them. Being composed of delegates from every shop and untrammelled by obsolete rule of law, we claim to represent the true feeling of the workers. We can act immediately according to the merits of the case and the desire of the rank and file.[24]

This was an important step forward. The CWC provided a model which militant workers across Britain would follow over the course of the war, laying the basis for independent rank and file organisation within the existing trade unions.

A year later the CWC was split on the question of dilution and was defeated by the government. Its leaders were either jailed along with John Maclean or deported from Clydeside, throwing the organisation into abeyance for over a year. But by the end of 1916 and throughout the following year similar stewards' organisations sprang up in the other major industrial centres. The Sheffield Workers' Committee, in particular, was even stronger than the Clyde organisation had been in 1915. The CWC was also revived again in 1917. These shop stewards and their new organisations would play a key role in the battles that lay ahead

Housing and rents

On Clydeside industrial unrest was accompanied by agitation against rent increases throughout 1915. Housing conditions in Glasgow were appalling, and even before the war working class areas were badly overcrowded, with an infant mortality rate among the worst in Europe. All the tenements were privately owned, and the landlords opposed to municipal housing.

When the war started, workers flooded into Glasgow to work in munitions, and the racketeer landlords started to raise rents and apply for eviction orders against tenants who couldn't pay. The hardest hit were the elderly, unemployed and the wives of soldiers, but rent rises made it difficult for even the employed to meet the landlords' demands.

The struggle against rent increases and evictions was most pronounced in the riverside districts of Partick and Govan, where most of the skilled workers employed in shipbuilding and engineering lived. Campaigns were initiated by local working class women, who formed tenants committees and housing associations. Some of the leading activists, like Helen Crawford and Mary Barbour, were members of the ILP. Indeed ILP activists, led by the Glasgow councillor John Wheatley, were prominent in demanding that the government freeze rents and municipalise housing.

Maclean supported these campaigns from the very beginning and encouraged other socialists to get involved. He had long been concerned with housing problems on Clydeside and had urged the BSP and other groups to work alongside Wheatley and the ILP on the issue.

One of the slanders spread about Maclean was that he was impossible to work with. Nothing could be further from the truth. Unlike many of his contemporaries on the left, Maclean was flexible; he was always prepared to work alongside and support other socialists on concrete issues, even when he was sceptical of their motives or held political differences, as was the case with the reformist ILP.

This did not mean that he was prepared to hide his politics, and he had fundamental disagreements with John Wheatley and the ILP. While they looked to parliament for change and framed their agitation accordingly, Maclean believed the rent struggle raised the question of working class power.

In the event, his distinctive contribution to the rent campaign proved to be the decisive one. He connected the anger over rents with the unrest in the factories and campaigned for strike action across the Clyde. He used the same techniques of factory gate agitation that he'd developed during the engineering strikes at the start of the war. He connected the immediate issue to the wider political situation, and he succeeded despite the abstention of the leading stewards on the CWC.

In May 1915 the first rent strike began in Govan when tenants refused to pay their increases. By August rent strikes were also taking place in Shettleston and Partick. In September a crowd of 2,000 prevented the eviction of one of the strike's leaders in Partick.

By October 30,000 tenants were withholding rents. There were local demonstrations against the Sheriff Officers (bailiffs) every time they attempted an eviction, and it was the women who played the key role in physically stopping the evictions. In October a tremendous demonstration in St Enoch's Square in central Glasgow demanded that the government curb the rent racketeers, but the government was not willing to act and instead an official Committee of Enquiry was set up to discuss the matter.

Then, on 17 November, strike action in the shipyards ended the need for Committees of Enquiry. Eighteen munitions workers were summoned to court for non-payment of rent in an attempt by the landlords to have their wages deducted at source. As a result all the Govan shipyard workers from the Fairfield, Stephens, and the Harland and Wolff yards downed tools and marched to the court in solidarity. En route they stopped at Lorne Street primary school in Kinning Park, where John Maclean was teaching under threat of dismissal for his anti-war activities. The shipyard workers carried him shoulder high through the streets and he addressed a demonstration of 10,000 outside the court. Maclean spoke on behalf of the strikers, making it clear that there would be no return to work until the charges were dropped. The meeting also agreed that Maclean would send a telegram to prime minister Asquith stating that:

This demonstration of Clyde munitions workers requests the government to state not later than Saturday first, that it forbids any rent increase during the period of the war and failing this, a general strike will be called on Monday, November 22nd.[25]

Victory

The sheriff, facing intense pressure, persuaded the landlord to drop the case. Fearing the consequences of a potential strike throughout the munitions industry, the government immediately introduced a Rent Restriction Act, capping rents all over Britain at their pre-war levels. 17 November 1915 must surely rank as one of the high points of British working class history. That night working class areas in Glasgow celebrated a spectacular victory.

The strike and demonstration outside the sheriff's court brought Maclean to the attention of a much wider audience. But it was also his last day as a schoolteacher. He was sacked by Govan School Board and for the rest of his life he was a professional revolutionary.

The following day he began his first spell as a political prisoner. Two months earlier he had been charged under the Defence of the Realm Act for making a seditious anti-war speech at Shawlands Cross in Glasgow. But because the case was heard on the day after the victorious rent strike, the authorities were careful not to make Maclean a martyr. The sheriff passed what looked like a very mild sentence for an act of treason—a £5 fine or five days in jail. Maclean refused to pay the fine and so spent five days in Duke Street prison.

A number of pits in the Lanarkshire coalfield struck in protest at his sacking and imprisonment. The shop stewards at Weir's also passed a resolution calling for a district levy of engineering workers to maintain Maclean as a political organiser and to demand his reinstatement as a school teacher.

7

The limits of trade unionism

The BSP newspaper *Justice* was controlled by Hyndman and the pro-war faction of the party. In late 1915 Maclean launched *The Vanguard* as the newspaper of the Glasgow BSP, which espoused a clear anti-war position. Writing in *The Vanguard*, Maclean emphasised the position of power which workers now held, and argued for political strike action to stop the war: "Capitalism, that is the right to rob the creators of wealth, must be killed and it can be done in twelve solid months, starting any time, if but the workers are ready".[26]

Peter Petroff, who had been an active member of the BSP's anti-war wing in London, moved back to Glasgow to assist Maclean. In successive issues of *The Vanguard* he concentrated on the Zimmerwald conference, held by anti-war socialists in Europe in September 1915. Petroff called for the creation of a new Socialist International, and hailed the Zimmerwald group as a welcome step in that direction. He also encouraged Maclean to directly confront Hyndman's old guard section of the BSP.

Petroff had a better knowledge of the BSP and of the wider European socialist movement than John Maclean. He was in regular contact with Trotsky and wrote articles for Trotsky's newspaper. Through his contact with the European revolutionary movement, Petroff helped Maclean to realise that his own revolutionary opposition to the war was shared by other European socialists.

For Maclean, the events of 1915 represented a major advance in working class consciousness. He argued that the rent strike was the first stage in the development of the political strike, which would eventually force an end to the war. Maclean's leading article in *The Vanguard* of December 1915 argued that:

> It should be noted that the rent strike on the Clyde is the first step towards the political strike so frequently resorted to on the continent. We rest assured that our comrades in the various workplaces will incessantly urge this aspect on their workmates, and so prepare the ground for the next great counter move of our class in the raging class warfare—raging more than ever during the Great Unrest period of three years ago.[27]

Syndicalism

But Maclean was also conscious of the weaknesses of the movement. He had been intimately involved in the rent struggle and maintained close contact with the CWC, and while he'd encouraged its formation and welcomed it as a positive step forward, he was becoming aware of the political limitations of its leadership. Crucial among these was its failure to bring wider political issues onto the shop floor. Instead the leaders of the shop stewards concentrated on narrow trade union issues for fear of dividing the movement. Yet many regarded themselves as revolutionary socialists.

During the rent campaign munitions workers struck against the landlords, and these solidarity strikes were a decisive factor in the campaign's success. But most of the CWC leaders played no role in the calls for industrial action. This angered Maclean, and he criticised the syndicalist position, which divorced politics from economics. He knew instinctively that such a separation would make it easier for the government to take the offensive against working class organisation. At the end of the rent strike Maclean wrote that:

Whether the Clyde Workers' Committee as constituted today is able or willing to cope with the situation is doubtful; but it is just as well to give it a further chance with the added support of miners and railwaymen. However, just as this unofficial committee views with suspicion the official committees of the various unions, and attempts to act as a driving force, we warn our comrades that they ought to adopt the same attitude and see that it pushes ahead. If it still clings on to academic discussions and futile proposals, it is their business to take the initiative into their own hands as they did in the case of the rents strike.[28]

Maclean's collaboration with Petroff focused him politically, and together they challenged the CWC to channel industrial discontent into political opposition to the war. But the long tradition of separating industrial militancy and revolutionary politics was difficult to overcome. Maclean rowed with the leading lights on the CWC, attacking them for their failure to put anti-war agitation to the fore, while they in turn dismissed his ideas as unrealistic and a threat to rank and file unity in the workshops. Harry McShane recalled that:

John Maclean had great hopes that the Glasgow rent strike heralded the development of political strikes in Britain. We had read about the mass political strikes in Russia before the war and we knew Rosa Luxemburg's *The Mass Strike*. But in Britain the next struggle was by the engineers against dilution—a very difficult fight for socialists who had always been opposed to craft trade unionism and advocated industrial unions. The CWC led the struggle against dilution, and John Maclean fell out with the leaders. He was opposed to the way the socialists on the committee were behaving and I agreed with him. John argued that the main struggle was against the war. Most of the stewards were anti-war socialists, but they had submerged their politics in workshop struggles and were not mentioning the war inside the factories. Willie Gallacher's conduct in particular angered Maclean. At the end of 1915 Willie came to speak at Bath Street, where the meetings were at the centre of our anti-war fight. He did not mention the war at all. John Maclean criticised him openly, asking: "How could any man calling himself a socialist speak at a meeting and not refer to the war that is raging in Europe?"[29]

1916: Lloyd George visits Glasgow

In order to win the war against Germany, the government had to win the war in the factories, and that meant upping the stakes. The prospect of conscription was being openly discussed, but the key issue was the cabinet's determination to achieve a rapid expansion in arms production through the Dilution of Labour Scheme. At the end of 1915 they resolved to defeat the CWC, by force if necessary.

Dilution could be seen either as something that concerned only craftsmen, or as part of a general attack on working class organisation, and to their credit the revolutionaries on the CWC saw dilution as a menace to organised labour and attempted to transcend sectionalism in their resistance to it. But their refusal to campaign against the war meant that they adopted a strategy which allowed the government to isolate the resistance.

At the end of 1915 the leaders of the CWC issued a leaflet explaining that the committee had been formed "for the purposes of concentrating the whole forces of the Clyde area against the Munitions Act". The aim was "simply and purely defensive", to protect hard-won trade union rights from erosion by wartime legislation.

The majority of the committee were revolutionary syndicalists. Led by Willie Gallacher and Johnny Muir, a member of the SLP, they decided that they would only accept dilution in return for nationalisation and workers' control.

Their two most important principles were that, firstly, wages should not be determined by sex, previous training, or experience, but solely by the work performed; and, second, that a workers' committee be elected, with the power to ensure that these agreements were carried out.

Maclean argued from a much more radical position. Before the war he had favoured dilution, believing that the ASE needed to expand its membership to include the unskilled and semi-skilled workers who were increasing in number as new technology was introduced. This had been his position from the time of the Singers strike in 1912, and this was the position now being adopted by the leadership of the CWC.

But in 1915, in the context of a war economy, Maclean opposed dilution because it meant more arms production for the war effort. As he told Willie Gallacher, the chairman of the CWC, "It's a contradiction to oppose the war, while negotiating with the government about how quickly and cheaply the weapons for the war can be produced".[30]

The reformist ILP faction on the CWC, represented by Davy Kirkwood, convenor of shop stewards at Beardmore's Parkhead Forge, argued for a negotiated dilution settlement. Kirkwood's proposal had been drawn up behind the scenes by his mentor, ILP councillor John Wheatley, later to become MP for Shettleston. The rest of the CWC were unaware that this had been done in collaboration with the government's dilution commissioners on the Clyde, who were sympathetic to the ILP proposal.

The political differences between Maclean's position and that of the leadership emerged at a crucial meeting of the CWC in December 1915. The Maclean group, represented by Petroff and James MacDougall, called for a complete stoppage of munitions production. Maclean arrived late at the meeting to find that his supporters had already been expelled by the chair, Willie Gallacher, who had refused to allow the proposal for a strike against the war to be put to the meeting.

Events now began to move quickly as the government seized the initiative. Lloyd George arranged to visit Clydeside, believing he could win the rank and file over. The assumption was that the "Welsh Wizard", as he was known, would tour the key workplaces and negotiate a breakthrough on dilution by dint of his personal charisma and political acumen.

Lloyd George humiliated

His visit turned into a personal humiliation. The CWC stewards, armed with their demands, refused to negotiate with him on a piecemeal, plant by plant basis. He turned up at Albion Motors to find that the workforce refused to meet or talk with him. Davy Kirkwood ignored the CWC's stand and met with him at Parkhead forge to discuss the ILP's proposals. On the following day Lloyd George met the rest of the CWC and no agreement was reached.

Lloyd George hoped to be able to negotiate over the heads of the stewards and convince the rank and file. On Christmas day, not then a holiday in Scotland, he addressed a large rally of engineering workers in the St Andrews Concert Hall in Glasgow. The audience was incredibly hostile and the meeting was essentially commandeered by the Clyde Workers' Committee. As Maclean reported in *The Vanguard*, "Seldom has a prominent politician, a leading representative of the governing classes, been treated with so little respect".[31]

However, the cabinet and the Ministry of Munitions had already made contingency plans to deal with the situation should Lloyd George's overtures fail, and they now brought these into effect.

The government offensive

Early in the spring of 1916 the government and the bosses combined to launch a major offensive against the leaders of the movement. This offensive was coordinated by the arms magnate Sir William Weir. As yet the Clydesiders had built few links with the rest of the country. The government would now take advantage of this weakness to isolate the shop stewards movement and impose dilution on the Clyde. The plan was to arrest, jail or deport the leaders, and to suppress the popular socialist press.

The government knew that by taking immediate action against the leading members of the CWC they might provoke a strike, and so they decided to begin their repression by focusing on safer targets. Peter Petroff and his wife were interned under the Defence of the Realm Act in January 1916. This neatly coincided with a xenophobic article in Hyndman's *Justice* which asked, "Who and what is Peter Petroff?"—advising the workers on Clydeside that he was a suspicious Russian troublemaker.

Forward, the mildly left wing newspaper of the ILP, was raided and, for a brief period, banned, while Maclean's *Vanguard* was seized and never appeared again for the duration of the war. Maclean himself was arrested in February on charges of sedition. In the same month police raided the SLP's headquarters and smashed the printing presses of the CWC newspaper, *The Worker*.

In the week that Maclean was arrested a unilateral dilution agreement was signed with the Dilution Commissioners by ILP member Davy Kirkwood on behalf of the workforce at Beardmore's Parkhead Forge. This broke the common front of the Clyde Workers' Committee.

The failure of the CWC to act encouraged the government to step up its repression, and two of its key leaders, Gallacher and Muir, were arrested, along with Walter Bell of the SLP. They were charged with sedition under the Defence of the Realm Act and were initially refused bail. When 10,000 munitions workers stopped work it was agreed to release them until their trial.

At this point the management at Beardmore's, with the prior approval of the cabinet, reneged on its side of the deal with Kirkwood. He and all the other shop stewards were denied right of access to every section of the plant, curtailing effective union organisation in the largest workplace on the Clyde. The workers at Parkhead and a few other plants struck in protest, but the widespread hostility towards Kirkwood's "go it alone" stance made it hard to spread the action—particularly in the absence of such a call from the CWC. While the question of solidarity hung in the balance the government rounded up all the key leaders.

Kirkwood and the leading stewards at Parkhead Forge, along with Arthur McManus and four other leading militants at Weir's, were dragged from their beds in the middle of the night and deported from Glasgow. The press was banned, under the Defence of the Realm Act, from reporting the deportations for over a week. Despite Kirkwood's moderation, he was too prominent to be left alone, as the government was out to break reformist resistance to the war economy, as well as revolutionary opposition to the war itself.

This was a make or break point moment for the struggle. If the CWC had called for a coordinated stoppage in protest against the Parkhead dilution agreement and the deportations, it could have inflicted a serious defeat on the government and reasserted its authority. A motion calling for such a strike was actually proposed at a CWC meeting but the chairman, Willie Gallacher, ruled it out of order.

Maclean and the leaders jailed

The trials took place in Edinburgh over April and May. Maclean appeared first, facing six indictments including incitement to strike against conscription, and for appealing to soldiers to lay down their arms. Lord Strathclyde imposed an exemplary sentence of three years penal servitude. Maclean would remain in prison until the summer of 1917.

Gallacher and Muir were both sentenced to 12 months and Bell received a three-month sentence. The government now refused to make any concessions on dilution to the CWC—even refusing to meet a deputation. Over the course of May, Jack Smith, the convenor at Weir's, received an 18-month sentence, and both Jimmy Maxton of the ILP and James MacDougall, Maclean's right hand man, were sentenced to a year.

The repression deprived the Clydeside working class of its leadership and silenced Maclean for over two years. The militant mood subsided, and resistance to dilution collapsed. The smashing of the CWC was a terrible defeat, but it was not decisive. The events reverberated throughout the factories and made an indelible impression on thousands of workers who had previously been indifferent to politics. While the struggle on Clydeside may have been in temporary abeyance, resistance soon spread to other munitions centres.

Mythology and the Labour left

A myth has grown up around this period, suggesting a close connection between the Clydeside MPs of the ILP, elected in 1922, and the wartime militancy associated with John Maclean and the Clyde Workers' Committee. This claim is quite unjustified. The ILP's Glasgow newspaper, *Forward*, gained some notoriety when one issue was banned, but as its editors pointed out:

> Looking through the files of *Forward* we can find no hint of incitement… Neither before or during the strike did we publish a single line about it…we declared in our issue of 20th March we should not touch the subject of strikes during the war.[32]

With the sole exception of Maxton, who was a pacifist, the ILP on Clydeside either adopted *Forward*'s position, or, like Kirkwood and Wheatley, worked to prevent strikes. In his autobiography, *My Life of Revolt*,

Davy—later Lord—Kirkwood describes what he did on the day the government commissioners arrived to impose dilution:

> We were all scared as the thundering masses of Germans tramped their way towards the coasts. That night I went to John Wheatley... In 30 minutes he drafted the scheme, which became the basis for the whole of Great Britain and worked perfectly till the end of the war...the extremists attacked us for having agreed to the increased production. John Maclean made me the theme of innumerable speeches.[33]

The truth is that Kirkwood and Wheatley sabotaged the position of the Clyde Workers' Committee, and unlike John Maclean none of the Clydeside ILP, with the exception of James Maxton, believed in striking against the war.

Conscription spreads the struggle

Lloyd George's victory over the Clydeside shop stewards' movement led to his promotion from munitions minister to secretary of state for war in the National Coalition government. David Lloyd George was a corrupt bigot and a warmonger. He backed the ruthless suppression of the 1916 Easter Rising in Dublin, including the summary execution of James Connolly and the other Republican leaders. In 1916 he imposed conscription to ensure the flow of cannon fodder to the front, and he ordered the Battle of the Somme, in which over a million were slaughtered. But while Lloyd George wallowed in bloodshed, revulsion to the war grew among the population.

In October 1916 Leonard Hargreaves, a fitter working at the Vickers munitions plant in Sheffield, was conscripted into the army despite a government pledge not to draft skilled munitions workers. After the horrors of the Somme conscription was tantamount to a death sentence, and yet the leaders of Hargreave's union, the ASE, refused to act.

The Sheffield shop stewards' movement, through the efforts of militants such as J T Murphy, who worked at Vickers, organised mass meetings to demand that Hargreaves be returned to civil life. When the authorities refused, the shop stewards moved swiftly and 12,000 Sheffield engineers downed tools. Motorcycle delegations were sent out across the country to win national support for the strike. Within three days the action had spread to other centres, and the government relented. As a result of this struggle, shop stewards' organisations were built throughout the Sheffield engineering industry.

In March 1917 10,000 workers took strike action in Barrow. In May the largest unofficial strike movement of the war began in Rochdale. This was a strike to prevent the extension of dilution to commercial contracts. The strike spread rapidly throughout the Manchester area and then to Sheffield, Rotherham and Coventry. More than 200,000 workers were involved.

As a result of this strike, the Shop Stewards' and Workers' Committee Movement established a National Advisory Council (NAC) to act as a reporting centre for the movement up and down the country. But while this was a step forward the NAC, as its name implied, held no executive power. This was deliberate, because most of the leaders of the shop stewards' movement were opposed to the idea of a centralised national leadership and insisted on local autonomy. This syndicalist prejudice would hamstring the movement in the coming battles against the war.

8

The end of tsarism

John Maclean was imprisoned in April 1916, just two weeks before the Easter Rising in Dublin. Lenin regarded the rising as the first real blow against both the war and the British Empire. Like James Connolly, Maclean's stand against the war brought him to the attention of the European revolutionary movement. Trotsky, writing for the Russian journal *Nashe Slovo*, reported that, "The Scottish soldiers smashed the Dublin barricades but in Scotland itself coalminers are rallying round the red banner raised by John Maclean".[34]

The BSP's Easter conference saw the decisive defeat of the Hyndman faction. They promptly left the party, taking the newspaper, *Justice*, with them. The BSP now adopted a pacifist position, while the imprisoned Maclean was elected to the executive for the first time and a campaign was launched for his release.

Early in 1917 news of the February Revolution and the overthrow of the tsarist regime in Russia gave tremendous inspiration and encouragement to the working class movement in Britain. On May Day 70,000 marched through Glasgow in solidarity. At the end of May 90,000 marched to Glasgow Green to protest against the decision to grant Lloyd George the freedom of the city, and to demand Maclean's release. Two hundred Russian sailors left their warship at anchor on the Clyde to join the march.

In June the All-Russian Congress of Workers' and Soldiers' Deputies sent fraternal greetings to "the brave fighter for the International, Comrade Maclean, and expresses their hopes that the new rise of international solidarity will bring him liberty".[35]

With the prisoners and deportees from the dilution struggle of 1915 back in the factories, the shop stewards' movement on the Clyde began to revive. Mass agitation led to Maclean's release in June 1917, after serving half of his three-year sentence.

The immediate impact of war had been to reduce strike days to virtually nil in 1914. When Maclean was jailed and the Clyde Workers' Committee was smashed in early 1916, it looked as if the nascent resistance movement had been contained by government repression. By the time of his release it was a very different picture. Throughout Britain a general revival of working class confidence had taken place, and class struggle was rising. This process was accelerated by the news of the February Revolution in Russia.

Although 5 million workers were away in the army, Britain's trade union membership was growing dramatically and the number of strikes and strike days lost was increasing. This was at a time when strikers had to take on the police, the army, the courts, the trade union officials and the Labour Party, as well as their bosses.

When Maclean returned to Glasgow in the autumn of 1917, he soon threw himself into renewed political activity. By early November his weekly class in Glasgow was attracting 500 workers, with 100 attending in Govan, 125 in Greenock and 300 miners attending in Lanarkshire.

The war after the war

It was for this working class audience that Maclean wrote his pamphlet *The War after the War* in the winter of 1917. This excellent introduction to economics uses Marx's theory of value to explain the connection between the assault on working class living standards and war. It explained why ending the current war on capitalist terms could only lead to an intensification of class struggle and further wars. The pamphlet also introduces the notion that the US will become the world's next leading power:

> We see preparations for this economic war, this war after the war. Every other capitalist country is doing the same, especially the United States, which has now passed from being a borrowing to being a lending country. It is getting a foothold in South and Central America and is manoeuvring with Japan for a firmer grip over the economic life of China.[36]

He would later develop this view further, speculating that, "In 15 years' time we may have the first great war bursting out in the Pacific—America v Japan."

Then came the breakthrough that made everything else seem possible—the Bolshevik Revolution in Russia in October 1917. Willie Gallacher recalls how:

> Maclean became a driving dynamo of energy, driving, always driving towards his goal. The work done by Maclean in the winter of 1917-18 has never been equalled by anyone.[37]

A month before the workers of Russia seized power, Lenin had written that:

> There can be no doubt that the end of September marked the beginning of a new period in the history of the Russian Revolution and, very probably, of the world revolution. The world working class revolution was first begun with engagements by isolated combatants, representing with unequalled courage, all the honest elements of "official" socialism—Liebknecht in Germany, Adler in Austria, Maclean in England [sic]; such are the best known of these isolated heroes who assumed the heavy task of precursors of the revolution.[38]

This was why Liebknecht, Adler and Maclean were elected, along with Lenin and Trotsky, as honorary presidents of the first All-Russian Congress of Soviets and why, at the beginning of 1918 Maclean was appointed Bolshevik Consul in Glasgow.

1918

In January 1918 the leadership of the British Shop Stewards' Movement finally decided to call for a national strike in an effort to force the government to start peace negotiations. A number of factors led them to move for action to halt the war: the impact of the October Revolution; the bloody stalemate on the western front; and acute food shortages at home. Despite a sizeable campaign and huge meetings of engineering workers threatening strike action, the actual strike did not materialise. At the last moment the skilled engineers drew back from their challenge to the state, opting instead for a militant, but highly sectional, demand for the continued exemption of skilled workers from military conscription.

The shop stewards' movement had developed between 1915 and 1918, when the war was still the dominant political issue. Yet, with few exceptions, the stewards were reluctant to raise the issue of opposition to the war inside the factories for fear of losing support, even though many of them were both anti-war and anti-capitalist. J T Murphy was one of the key leaders of the movement, and in 1917 he wrote one of the key pamphlets of the shop stewards movement, *The Workers' Committee*, but it never even mentioned the war.

The engineering workers could have served as the vanguard of a struggle to end the war and challenge British capitalism, but their power was never marshalled for this purpose. In Glasgow, where Maclean had consistently denounced the war, the call was taken up with enthusiasm. At the end of January a huge meeting in Glasgow supported the CWC's call for strike action, but there was no national organisation and no mass party like the Bolsheviks advocating revolutionary struggle inside the workplaces. The Glasgow stewards did not feel strong enough to act alone.

In February 1918 the National Advisory Committee of the Shop Stewards' and Workers' Committee Movement published its position:

> If we could only be certain that the German workers would follow suit, we would have no hesitation in calling for an immediate policy of down tools and damn the consequences. But we are not in touch with our fellow workers in Germany. It may be that they are willing to do the bidding of their warlords.[39]

Within days of this article going to print, 400,000 German workers struck against the war.

The accuser of capitalism

In 1918 Maclean became the subject of close surveillance by the security services and a topic of discussion in Lloyd George's cabinet. In February the general officer of the army in Scotland outlined his fears about the situation in Glasgow and requested that Maclean's parole be cancelled or a renewed prosecution be brought against him. At the beginning of April 1918 Maclean was invited to do a speaking tour of the Durham coalfield, and wherever he went huge crowds turned out to hear him advocate revolution. He had just returned to Glasgow when he was arrested once again for sedition. His trial was fixed for 9 May and he was refused bail.

Before his arrest Maclean had been arguing that the Clydeside workers should strike against the war on May Day. After his arrest the Glasgow May Day Committee decided, for the first time ever, to hold the annual demonstration on Wednesday 1 May. It was a tremendous display of working class unity. One hundred thousand stayed away from work and there was a solidarity march to Duke Street jail, where Maclean was awaiting trial.

Maclean was brought to trial in Edinburgh in May and charged with sedition. The range and extent of the charges against him, and the manner in which he conducted his own defence, showed the extent to which he had rejected the old values of the Second International and had adopted the Bolshevik position of revolutionary defeatism and workers' power.

He used the dock of the High Court in Edinburgh as a platform to speak out against the capitalist system, and ended with an appeal to the working class to destroy it:

> No government is going to take from me my right to protest against wrong... I am not here as the accused, I am here as the accuser of capitalism, dripping with blood from head to foot.[40]

The judge sentenced him to five years penal servitude, and this immediately provoked a massive campaign for Maclean's release. Lenin, in his speech to the Russian Trade Union Congress, said:

> The British government imprisoned him because he exposed the object of the war and spoke out against the criminal nature of British imperialism—and this time not only as a Scottish schoolteacher, but also as the consul of the Soviet Republic.[41]

9

The post-war storm

The Russian Revolution initiated a wave of revolt across Europe. Revolutionary regimes were established in Hungary, Bavaria, Finland and Latvia. Both the German Kaiser and the Emperor of Austria were overthrown. Germany was the focal point of unrest. In October 1918 the German fleet mutinied and the army began to turn against its officers. Duncan Hallas has written that:

> By 4 November revolutionary feeling in the port of Kiel was at fever heat...the high command and the officers of the navy surrendered, while some on the Battleship *Koenig* and other vessels were killed. The sailors had become masters of the situation and army units in the area joined them.
>
> In Kiel there was only one authority—the elected Council of Workers, Sailors and Soldiers Deputies. From Kiel the rebellion spread to Hamburg, Bremen and Cuxhaven. On the night of 8 November it was learned in Berlin that the rebellion had triumphed with little or no resistance in Hanover, Magdeburg, Cologne, Stuttgart, Frankfurt, Brunswick, Oldenburg and other cities .At eight o'clock on the morning of 9 November the general strike broke out in Berlin itself.[42]

The Kaiser fled and the German workers, through their council of deputies, found themselves in power. The Armistice was signed on 11 November and the war was ended by working class revolution. This spirit of revolt also extended to the victorious states.

Britain on the brink of revolution

In October 1918, while Maclean was still in prison, a general election was called. The Gorbals Labour Party chose him as their candidate, ignoring the fierce opposition of Labour's national executive. The government panicked and agreed to his release. He was freed in December.

In 1919 the class struggle would rise to unprecedented heights—the nearest Britain has yet come to social revolution. In a secret memorandum Lloyd George lamented that:

> The whole of Europe is filled with the spirit of revolution. There is a deep sense not only of discontent, but of anger and revolt amongst the workmen. The whole existing order in its political, social and economic aspects is questioned by the masses of the population from one end of Europe to the other. [43]

Likewise, Field Marshall Sir Henry Wilson told the cabinet that in his view, "A Bolshevik rising was likely".[44] The head of Special Branch, Basil Thomson, warned that, "February 1919 was the high watermark of revolutionary danger".[45]

Disaffection was rampant throughout the armed forces. In January 20,000 soldiers mutinied in Calais, demanding repatriation. Another 10,000 soldiers mutinied at Folkestone and refused to return to France, and a further 4,000 demonstrated in solidarity at Dover. In the same week 1,500 soldiers at Osterley Park seized lorries and drove them to London, where they demonstrated outside the war office. There was a mutiny on board HMS *Kilbride*, when sailors hauled the red flag up the masthead and declared, "Half the navy are on strike and the other half soon will be".[46] In May a mass strike by policemen took place in London and Liverpool. Clearly the state could not rely on military force during the crisis of 1919.

When revolution had broken out in Russia at the start of 1917, the Bolsheviks had 20,000 members and a cadre that had been schooled through 14 years of independent revolutionary activity under illegal conditions. It had a thriving press that was eagerly read and supported financially by militant workers.

Maclean was an enthusiastic supporter of Lenin and the Bolsheviks. In 1919 he was the most consistent advocate of the notion that the British working class could take power. He was a brave, energetic and talented individual who possessed a considerable amount of respect within the working class movement. But he had no organisation, and his direct supporters could be counted in single figures. He did not have a party, or even the beginnings of a party, like the Bolsheviks. Had such a party existed it could have grown exponentially during 1919, with the ruling class on the ropes and everything to play for.

Amid this mood of post-war militancy the CWC held a conference of shop stewards in shipbuilding and engineering on 5 January 1919, to launch the 40 hour strike for a limit on the working week. This was seen as a way of forcing the employers to absorb rising unemployment, stemming from demobilisation and the end of the munitions boom. John Maclean made desperate appeals for the engineers to link up with the miners, who were themselves about to launch a national struggle. In 1919 the miners were demanding a 30 percent wage increase, a reduction in the working week and the nationalisation of the pits.

Because of the urgent need for coal, the miners had real weight and they were in an extremely militant mood. The issue of nationalisation was being forced upon the coal owners and the government by the threat of mass action from below. Maclean understood that this represented a tremendous political attack on the ruling class. .

Throughout January he had been campaigning for the Miners' Reform Movement in the Scottish and South Wales coalfields. In that same month the Miners' Federation

Conference was being held in Southport, so Maclean spent a week in the Lancashire coalfields organising unofficial committees in preparation for what he hoped would be a national coal strike.

He was therefore not present as the key events of the 40 hour strike unfolded in Glasgow. He urged the engineers to wait until the miners struck, and to then throw their weight behind an all-out challenge to the ruling class. The CWC ignored Maclean and did not bother to contact the rest of the National Shop Stewards' Movement. Although Maclean believed the 40 hour strike was premature, once it was in motion he campaigned hard for its success:

> Some of us would have preferred the miners to lead off but as we all ought to know, historical events never start and shape themselves as we plan them. The strike on the Clyde has been precipitated by general discontent expressed at hosts of workshop and union meetings and by the anxiety of the union officials not to let the matter slip out of their hands, lest they be supplanted by industrial unionism. Into the conflict then, let this be the class war started at last.[47]

Maclean's comments on the anxiety of union officials were accurate. The dispute was controlled by the STUC and the executive of the Glasgow Trades Council, and although the CWC was included on the organising committee, it was hamstrung by officialdom. The strike committee chairman was Manny Shinwell, a trade union official and a member of the ILP. Before the strike began he publicly stressed the reformist aims of the strike's leadership: "This movement is NOT revolutionary in character. It is attributable solely and entirely to the fear of possible unemployment".[48]

The 40 hour strike
The 40 hour strike ranks as a key moment in the development of the revolutionary movement in Britain. The abiding

symbol of Red Clydeside is the raising of the red flag in Glasgow's George Square during the strike. But Lloyd George and Winston Churchill had prepared for the worst. Under secret cabinet orders, 10,000 troops had been placed on standby for imminent dispatch to Clydeside if necessary.

The strike began at the end of January, and the Clyde valley ground to a halt. Forty thousand struck on the first day, and this number soon rose. The government knew that a workers' victory would represent a disaster for the ruling class. But the union officials were more in control than had been the case during the war and their aims were far from revolutionary. The cabinet met to assess matters and Churchill, then minister of labour, urged caution. The army command explained that a massive show of force was risky since the army was unreliable: "Once we had a well disciplined and ignorant army, whereas now we have an army educated and ill disciplined".[49] Churchill concluded the best strategy was "a judicious use of force at an opportune moment",[50] combined with support from the trade union leaders.

After about a week there was a virtual general strike on Clydeside, with over 100,000 out indefinitely. Flying pickets consisting of thousands had gone from factory to factory and closed everything in their path. And despite the leadership's lack of effort in spreading the action, Belfast and Barrow were paralysed too. The strike was if anything even more successful in Belfast than it was on the Clyde.

The key moment was "Bloody Friday". On the morning of Friday 31 January 35,000 strikers and unemployed soldiers marched into Glasgow's George Square demanding a reduction in hours to absorb the unemployed. Reporters from the major British and European newspapers—including the young war poet Siegfried Sassoon—were there to witness the event. The authorities, under Churchill's guidance, deliberately provoked the confrontation that followed.

John Maclean

The police baton-charged the demonstration, but the crowds fought back and drove off the police. The strikers then marched to a rally in Glasgow Green. Willie Gallacher, the chairman of the CWC, was bludgeoned by police and then arrested for incitement to riot. This provocation, planned by the cabinet, was the "opportune moment" Churchill had been waiting for. The strike leaders were seized, and on that same evening the troops held on standby were flooded into the city, equipped with tanks and machine guns.

An eyewitness gave the following account:

Next morning Glasgow was like an armed camp. Throughout the night trainloads of young English soldiers had been brought to the city—young lads of 19 or so who had no idea of where they were or why they were there. The authorities did not dare use the local regiments billeted at Maryhill barracks, in case they supported the strikers. The whole city bristled with tanks and machine guns.[51]

The *Glasgow Herald* reported:

The panic of the civic and national authorities can only be explained thus—they actually believed a Spartacus uprising was planned to start in the city and they were prepared to suppress it at all costs.[52]

This was a decisive moment for the developing revolutionary movement in Britain. At this point the London electricians threatened to black out London, and engineers in Sheffield, Manchester, London and Tyneside were on the verge of walking out.

But once the army had been mobilised by the cabinet, coordinated attacks on the strike by the press and union officials were also implemented. The strike committees in Glasgow, London and Belfast—the three most militant areas—were suspended by their own union leaders, with their strike pay also suspended. The mass picketing was called off, on the understanding that an official national strike would be called. But this was merely a ruse by the union leaders. The strike petered out, with Glasgow turned into an armed camp, but according to Maclean the strike was defeated "more by lack of working class ripeness, than batons, tanks and machine guns"—and he was correct.

Mass picketing and demonstrations had demonstrated the potential power of the working class, but without clear-sighted revolutionary leadership that potential was wasted by the trade union leadership. In his book *Revolt on the Clyde* Willie Gallacher claimed, "We were leading a strike when we should have been leading a revolution. A rising was expected—a rising should have taken place".[53] But he was wrong. They were not leading a revolution, or at least not yet. If Gallacher and the local leadership had actually led the strike as revolutionaries, they could have won. Instead, they behaved as if the Clyde existed in isolation. It was linked to the shop stewards' organisations in Sheffield, London, Barrow, Belfast and all the mining centres across Britain. If they had maintained the mass picketing instead of calling it off when the army appeared; if they had marched the 35,000 demonstrators to Maryhill Barracks instead of Glasgow Green; and if they had sent delegations out to the coalfields and to England, they could have defeated a severely weakened ruling class.

After all, 1919 was a year of revolution across Europe and the year when the Irish War of Independence reached fever pitch. Victory for the 40 hour strike would have terrified an already worried British ruling class and opened up the road to revolution. In 1919 there were over one million miners in Britain, organised in the Miners' Federation. In pithead ballots they had voted overwhelmingly for an all-out strike in support of a 30 percent wage increase, a two-hour reduction in the working day, and nationalisation. Maclean believed the miners' struggle was the key issue because it had the potential to unite the whole of the working class in a confrontation with British capitalism. War-time profits meant that the coal owners could afford to make concessions on wages and conditions, but nationalisation on the miners' terms was a different matter. It was a political threat to the employer class, who wanted an end to the state interference necessitated by the war.

Lloyd George and the union leaders

With the war over and unemployment set to rise, the working class faced a stark choice between accepting sacrifices or challenging the priorities of capitalism. The outcome of the miners' struggle would swing the balance either way. The government was not in a strong position, so it played for time by proposing the establishment of a Royal Commission to look into the miners' demands. In his autobiography Nye Bevan recounts how the miners' leader, Robert Smillie, described to him a famous interview between Lloyd George and the trade union leaders of the Triple Alliance (an arrangement between the Miners' Federation, the transport union and the railway unions to support one another in the face of employers' attacks):

> Lloyd George sent for the leaders and they went, determined not to be talked over by the eloquent Welshman. "He was quite frank with us from the outset," said Bob Smillie. "He said to us, 'Gentlemen, you have fashioned, in the Triple Alliance of the unions represented by you, a most powerful instrument. I feel bound to tell you that we are at your mercy. The army is disaffected and cannot be relied upon. Trouble has already occurred in a number of camps. We have just emerged from a great war and the people are eager for the reward of their sacrifices but we are in no position to satisfy them. If you carry out your threat you will defeat us. But if you do,' asked Mr Lloyd George, 'have you

weighed the consequences? The strike will be in defiance of the government of the country and by its very success, will precipitate a constitutional crisis of the first importance. For if a force arises in the state which is stronger than the state itself, then it must be ready to take on the functions of the state or withdraw and accept the authority of the state. Gentlemen', asked the prime minister quietly, 'have you considered, and if you have, are you ready?' From that moment," said Smillie, "We were beaten and we knew it".[54]

The union leaders were terrified of the consequences and settled for an acceptance of the Sankey Coal Commission, which they tried to sell to the miners as a victory. Maclean saw the government's compromise as a trap to disarm the miners and avoid a confrontation it could not win. He argued "Governments never compromise unless they have to—now is the time to break British capitalism for good".[55] But the government strategy worked, thanks to the union leaders who sold the compromise to the rank and file. The Sankey Commission was a turning point in British working class history, for it delayed indefinitely one of the best opportunities to challenge the capitalist class. The union leaders had let the government off the hook.

Lloyd George and his cabinet recognised the conservative role played by the labour and trade union leaders. He knew that in periods of acute crisis they would stick with the status quo rather than risk revolution. As the Tory leader Bonar Law said, "Trade union organisation was the only thing between us and anarchy; without it our position was hopeless".[56]

The next major crisis for the government was a national railway strike. The railway workers were the most powerful group of all, but their leader, Jimmy Thomas, was an archetypal right winger. Try as he might, he could not stop a national strike breaking out in September 1919, but he did

John Maclean

manage to end it within nine days. The railway strike was followed by a strike of 65,000 foundry workers and a series of other disputes across the country. But each struggle was isolated, and the opportunity for an all-out confrontation with a vulnerable ruling class had been squandered. Had the Communist Party been formed in 1918 or early 1919, it could have taken advantage of a great opportunity. But it wasn't, and by 1920 the tide was already turning.

10

The retreat:
Maclean and the CPGB

Maclean believed that revolution was possible in 1919. Some commentators argue that this was simply wishful thinking, but any serious study of what happened proves that Maclean's was a realistic assessment. Even sections of the ruling class believed that their immediate future was in jeopardy.

Maclean had been one of the most persistent advocates of revolution, but he was also among the first to grasp that the balance of forces was shifting in favour of the bosses by the end of the year. By 1920 the post-war boom had ended. Rising unemployment sapped working class confidence, and the ruling class were on the offensive.

The self-confident workplace organisation which had been the heart of the working class movement was broken. On Clydeside unemployment among the engineers multiplied by a factor of 22, and in these conditions it was easy for management to weed out the militants. This process was replicated throughout the country. J T Murphy described the consequences:

> At Vickers in Sheffield it is questionable whether there is a single active shop steward or literature seller left in the place. They have practically all been cleared out under the cloak of unemployment. The same applies to many prominent people on the Clyde.[57]

Maclean's significance was that he connected his internationalism with the mass movement of workers on Clydeside and beyond. In their biography of Maclean, Brian Ripley and John McHugh explain the scale of his achievement:

It was because Maclean was so well versed in Marxism that he was able to approach the consequences of the Bolshevik Revolution with a degree of confidence, which few of his contemporaries on the left could match. Almost until his death he was able to apply himself to practical political problems with insight and realism. It needs emphasising that Maclean had no direct access to the works of Lenin, Luxemburg or any of the Marxist critics of Second International Marxism. The fact that he was able to develop his Marxism in ways that brought him close to those more august figures, while operating in such isolation is remarkable. Certainly he was better able than any of his British contemporaries to appreciate something of the flavour of Bolshevism without understanding its full meaning.[58]

Founding the Communist Party

However, as the movement subsided and the struggle declined, Maclean's base among working class militants disappeared. He began to search for a way forward. The great opportunity of 1919 had been missed because of the lack of revolutionary organisation within the working class. In 1920 the only option was to begin the process of building a party along Bolshevik lines. The potential for such an organisation existed among the militants who had led the rank and file struggles of the previous years.

With this in mind, and with the encouragement and assistance of Lenin and the Communist International, the Communist Party of Great Britain (CPGB) was launched in the summer of 1920. It is clear that those who came together in 1920-21 to form the new party were, for the most part, the best elements of the British working class movement. Yet Maclean, who could have contributed so much to the new organisation, refused to join. It was a serious mistake on his part.

A year earlier, during the upheavals of 1919, Maclean had been involved in a struggle within the BSP. At the party's annual conference in Sheffield, E C Fairchild, a pacifist who had taken over the leadership of the organisation in 1916, argued from an anti-Bolshevik position, calling for greater unity between the BSP and the Labour Party.

Maclean led the opposition to Fairchild. He was quite willing to support the BSP's affiliation with the Labour Party and the notion that socialists should contest elections. But Maclean argued in support of the Third International and for a rejection of the notion that socialism could be achieved through parliament. Instead he argued that the working class would have to directly seize power.

There is no doubt that Lenin and the Bolshevik leadership regarded Maclean as one of Britain's leading revolutionaries, and expected him to be a key figure in the new party. That's why the Communist International, when inviting 40 organisations throughout the world to join it in 1919, asked the BSP, and "particularly that tendency represented by Maclean", to take part.

Yet by the summer of 1920 Maclean was marginalised, and was eventually forced out of the BSP by the same individuals who would later played a crucial role in the negotiations leading to the formation of the CPGB. These were individuals with whom he'd had serious political disagreements over the war, and over their attitude to labourism. Maclean's daughter Nan Milton argues that he refused to join the Communist Party because he was already convinced of the need for Scottish independence and the formation of a separate Scottish Communist Party. But this is not the case. Maclean's argument with the leaders of the embryonic CPGB was well under way before he ever considered the notion of a Scottish Workers' Republic.

It was neither geographical nor national differences that kept Maclean out of the CPGB. Indeed, it was a fellow Scot, Willie Gallacher, who was the subject of Maclean's sharpest criticism. Maclean had a greater grasp of the political situation than any of the future leaders of the Communist Party. Unlike them he had developed, independently, Bolshevik ideas that they were now trying to learn parrot fashion. He was acutely aware of this, and doubted whether they were capable of providing revolutionary leadership. But even at this point it is not clear that Maclean had actually refused to join the CPGB.

Outmanoeuvred by Gallacher and Rothstein

There is plenty of evidence to show that Maclean was deliberately marginalised through the efforts of Theodore Rothstein and Willie Gallacher. Rothstein was a key figure in the negotiations to launch the CPGB and had been a leading member of the BSP during the war. Maclean did not trust Rothstein's judgement any more than he did Gallacher's—and with good reason.

In 1916 Lenin had attacked Rothstein because he continued to support the Second International. Even after 1917 he took a pacifist line on the war, calling for a negotiated peace rather than working class revolution. In his book, *The Revolutionary Movement*, Walter Kendall writes that "Rothstein does not seem to have declared for Bolshevism until after the October Revolution".[59]

When the last BSP conference was held Maclean tried to attend as a delegate, but the conference arrangements committee would not accept his credentials. From then on Maclean felt excluded from the negotiations that led to the formation of the CPGB. Maclean also alleged that Rothstein arranged for his secret expulsion from the BSP.

Understandably, Maclean was embittered by these events, especially when individuals like Gallacher accused him of mental imbalance caused by his time in prison. Maclean himself didn't help matters. He played into his opponents' hands by dismissing them out of hand and by allowing them to sideline him without a fight. The second congress of the

Communist International was held in Moscow in August 1920. Maclean was invited and wanted to attend, but he was denied a passport by the British government and refused to go illegally because he was the official Soviet consul in Britain. Lenin would not have been so intransigent.

The Communist International was disappointed by the limited success of the CPGB's launch and issued a call for renewed unity negotiations to pull in people like Maclean. Maclean ignored this resolution and set up a small socialist propaganda team. It was not until 1921 that he tried to rally support for a Scottish Communist Party. His eventual formation of a separate party in Scotland therefore stemmed primarily from his political differences with Gallacher and Rothstein, rather than from nationalist sentiment.

Though hostile to the leaders of the CPGB, Maclean remained committed to the Bolsheviks and to the Communist International. He was right to be critical of Gallacher and Rothstein, but it would have been far better for Maclean, and for the CPGB, had he joined with them and helped to develop the party's membership.

II

Socialist or nationalist?

Maclean's call for a Scottish Workers' Republic came in 1921, and he launched the Scottish Workers' Republican Party in 1923. Significantly, this took place in the aftermath of a major defeat for the working class movement, and serves as an indication of Maclean's frustration and isolation as a revolutionary. Maclean's close associate Harry McShane, who worked alongside him until 1922, described his attitude to Maclean's Scottish organisation:

> I felt a great deal of loyalty to John Maclean, but conscious that I was isolated, I knew I had to join an organisation. I joined the Communist Party in 1922. John formed the Scottish Workers' Republican Party in 1923, it had some people I didn't like—they'd never been to John's economic classes, they knew nothing about socialism or revolutionary work. Even if I hadn't joined the CPGB, I would never have joined with that crowd.[60]

Until this period Scottish nationalism had been of no significance to Maclean. Even his daughter Nan Milton, who wanted to paint him in nationalist colours, wrote, "There is little evidence that Maclean took the question of Scottish nationalism seriously until 1920." Throughout his entire political life Maclean had been preoccupied with the prospect of a British revolution. But the missed opportunity of 1919, and the retreat that followed in 1920, caused him to lose faith in the ability of a united British working class to achieve socialism. By the end of 1920 he began to turn, in desperation, to the notion of a Scottish workers' republic.

Opposition to empire

As one of the few socialists to have defended the 1916 Easter Rising, Maclean saw how the fight for independence in Ireland had shaken the British Empire, and he believed a similar fight for a Scottish workers' republic could challenge it further. But he underestimated the differences between Scotland and Ireland, and never took into account the contrasting roles played by the Scottish bourgeoisie and their Irish counterparts in relation to British imperialism. While the Irish were prepared to fight a war against British rule, the Scottish ruling class was a partner within the British Empire.

Maclean was also convinced that, now that Germany had been defeated, a new imperialist war between Britain and the United States was inevitable. This was an idea he'd first developed in 1918 and it was not as fanciful and improbable as it sounds today—it was a development that Trotsky had also considered.

It is important to place the republicanism of Maclean's final years in context. Unlike the nationalists who claim him, Maclean was "out for a workers' republic, created by the working class and based on a workers' soviet in Glasgow". This is a far cry from Scottish nationalism—a tradition which, unlike Irish republicanism, has never posed any kind of challenge to British imperialism. It must also be said that, while Maclean supported the Irish republican movement in its struggle against Britain, like James Connolly he argued for a socialist Ireland and criticised those Irish nationalists who wanted to subordinate class struggle to the notion of an all-class alliance:

> In no way can Maclean be claimed by the nationalists or by those on the Scottish left who believe that a Scottish parliament can bring socialism or fundamental change. Lenin, the leader of the Russian Revolution, argued that one strike is worth ten election victories. He understood that socialism

is about the working class liberating itself and transforming society from the bottom up.

Maclean had broken from the Second International and arrived at the same position as Lenin, rejecting the notion that socialism could come through parliament. After 1920 he called for a Glasgow soviet—a revolutionary workers' council based on workplace organisation—because he believed that the working class would have to directly confront the British state. When the struggle declined in England he thought it still possible to strike a blow at the British ruling class from Scotland, a blow delivered by the collective power of the working class that would weaken the British Empire, prevent the next war and trigger an international revolt:

> I hold that the British Empire is the greatest menace to the human race. The best interests of humanity can therefore be served by its break up. We can make Glasgow a Petrograd, a revolutionary storm centre second to none. A Scottish breakaway at this juncture would bring the empire crashing to the ground and free the waiting workers of the world... English labour is bound to respond to our call if we in Scotland strike out boldly for political conquest.[61]

His motivation was internationalist rather than nationalistic, but his reading of the situation was wrong. For once his estimation of the mood of the Clydeside working class was not based on his usual sober realism. The level of unemployment had risen dramatically, from 16 percent in 1920 to 25 percent in 1923. The militant workplace organisation that had provided the backbone of the Red Clyde was already broken, just as it had been broken elsewhere. His view that workers in Glasgow were ready to seize power in 1922 says more about his own isolation than it does about the actual balance of forces.

It was a shortcut to revolution, but like many shortcuts it proved to be a dead end. Even if Maclean's Glasgow Soviet had come to pass, the bloody defeat of the Dublin rising in 1916 should have taught him that a Red Glasgow would have to endure all the barbarism that the British state could muster, and only one thing could have saved a workers' Glasgow from certain defeat: solidarity from those very English cities that, Maclean now insisted, lagged behind the Scots.

Isolation

Maclean's isolation meant that, like many great socialists, he was unable to come to terms with a sudden, sharp reversal in the political situation. In the period after 1920 the key issue for socialists was how to stop the retreat, how to rebuild shop floor organisation, and how to revive working class confidence. Above all, it meant the building of the working class party along Bolshevik lines, in British conditions. Tragically, his refusal to join the Communist Party cut him off from the most class-conscious workers, and the one organisation which, despite its undoubted weaknesses, did face up to the task of rebuilding the working class movement.

It was a grave error, and both he and the Communist Party suffered for it. It isolated him from the working class movement, and deprived the Communist Party of the most talented and courageous socialist in Britain just as the General Strike of 1926 was approaching.

Maclean died of ill health and poverty in 1923, and to his great credit he remained a revolutionary right to the end. For the last two years of his life his political perspective failed to address the real problems of the working class movement. Despite being a keen supporter of Bolshevism, he failed to grasp the importance of Lenin's party and left nothing behind in the way of political organisation.

But these weaknesses cannot diminish his immense significance for socialists today. Throughout the 20th century British nationalism has dominated the Labour Party and the trade union bureaucracy, and the working class has paid

John Maclean

a terrible price. In 1926 the betrayal of the General Strike moved Trotsky to write that:

> If there were not a bureaucracy of the trade unions, then the police, the army, the courts, the lords, the monarchy would appear before the proletarian masses as nothing but pitiful ridiculous playthings. The bureaucracy of the trade unions is the backbone of British imperialism. It is by means of this bureaucracy that the bourgeoisie exists.[62]

John Maclean stands in opposition to this tradition, which has always accommodated to the "national interest". He was a revolutionary internationalist who saw the First World War for what it was—an imperialist conflict. He refused to be silenced and rallied the opposition to that war through his energy and courage. He shared Lenin's revolutionary defeatism and stood up in defence of Ireland's fight for independence. In 1915 he was among the very first on the British left to anticipate a new revolutionary International, and he was the most energetic supporter of the Bolshevik Revolution.

The fact that he fashioned his ideas in relative isolation and under severe state persecution marks him out as a great revolutionary. As an earlier biography explained, "Certainly what is distinctive about Maclean is not his 'Scottishness' but the 'non-Britishness' of his approach to political questions".[63]

Maclean's significance lies in his attempt to unite theory and practice. He worked tirelessly to connect his internationalism to real mass movements of workers. He came late to an understanding that socialism could only be achieved through workers' power and revolution, but he fought for that cause for the rest of his life. He cannot be understood in any other way.

Maclean's relevance today

Maclean's message about the necessity of revolution can appeal to a new generation looking for real change. His legacy stands in stark contrast to the tradition of labour reformism, which has dominated and constrained the British working class movement since his death. Under Tony Blair and Gordon Brown, New Labour embraced the market and governed in the interests of the rich and powerful. The betrayal of their own supporters and their eagerness to do the bidding of American imperialism in backing the "war on terror" have spread disillusionment and paved the way for the return of a Tory-led coalition and a cabinet of millionaires.

But with Osborne's voodoo economic strategy a proven failure and Cameron humiliated over Syria, the coalition government looks doomed. In terms of political representation, voters have little to choose between the mainstream political parties. All them are committed, in varying degrees, to continuing with austerity and neoliberalism and defending the free market—and that includes the SNP.

As capitalism plunges the world deeper into economic and ecological crisis, military conflict and social upheaval, the 21st century has begun just as the 20th century did. Lenin described it as an epoch of wars and revolutions. Maclean, like Lenin, was a revolutionary at a time when the future of capitalism hung in the balance. He stood for its overthrow by working people everywhere.

In May 1918, facing five years hard labour for inciting workers to transform war into revolution, he made his famous speech from the dock at the High Court in Edinburgh. In it he denounced the horrors of the capitalist system and appealed directly to ordinary working people:

> I am not here as the accused—I am here as the accuser of capitalism dripping with blood from head to foot. In the next five years there is going to be a great world trade depression and the respective governments must turn more and more to the markets of the world to get rid of their produce. And in 15 years time from the close of this war we are into the next war—if capitalism lasts we cannot escape it. My

appeal is to the working class. I appeal exclusively to them because they, and they alone, can bring about the time when the whole world will be in one brotherhood, on a sound economic foundation. That, and that alone, can be the means of bringing about a reorganisation of society. That can only be obtained when the people of the world get the world and retain the world.[64]

Maclean stood for international socialism and workers' power. Today his appeal is more relevant than ever. It cannot be allowed to rest passively in the history books.

Notes

1 Dave Sherry, *John Maclean*, first edition (SWP, 1998), p51.

2 John Swinney, BBC Scotland Interview, 2012.

3 P Berresford Ellis, *James Connolly: Selected Writings* (Penguin, 1975), p124.

4 Neil Davidson, "What is Scottish Independence For?" in Gregor Gall (ed), *Scotland's Road to Socialism: Time to Choose* (Scottish Left Review Press, 2013), p54.

5 John Maclean, *In the Rapids of Revolution*, edited by Nan Milton (Allison and Busby, 1978), p233.

6 Karl Marx and Frederick Engels, *On Britain* (Foreign Languages Publishing House, 1962), p582.

7 J T Murphy, *Preparing for Power* (Pluto Press, 1972), p116.

8 B J Ripley and J McHugh, *John Maclean* (Manchester University Press, 1989), p41.

9 Harry McShane, *Remembering John Maclean* (John Maclean Society, 1972), p2.

10 Ripley and McHugh, as above, p30.

11 Ripley and McHugh, as above, p52.

12 Ripley and McHugh, as above, p48.

13 Walter Kendall, *The Revolutionary Movement in Britain 1900-1921* (Weidenfeld & Nicholson, 1961), p89.

14 Duncan Hallas, *The Comintern* (Bookmarks, 1985), p14.

15 V I Lenin, *The War and the Second International* (International Publishers, 1932), p9.

16 Maclean, as above, p76.

17 Harry McShane and Joan Smith, *No Mean Fighter* (Pluto Press, 1978), p63.

18 Ray Challinor, *The Origins of British Bolshevism* (Croom Helm, 1977), p124.

19 McShane and Smith, as above, p64.

20 Willie Gallacher, *Revolt on the Clyde* (Lawrence & Wishart, 1936), p37.

21 Challinor, as above, p131.

22 Challinor, as above, p131.

23 James Hinton, *The First Shop Stewards Movement* (Allen & Unwin, 1973), p106.

24 "Fellow Workers", the Clyde Workers' Committee's first leaflet, November 1915.

25 Challinor, as above, p133.

26 Ripley and McHugh, as above, p86.

27 Maclean, as above, p86.

28 Maclean, as above, p86.

29 McShane and Smith, as above, p77.

30 Ripley and McHugh, as above, p88.

31 Challinor, as above, p136.

32 *Forward*, 5 February, 1916.

33 Tony Cliff and Donny Gluckstein, *The Labour Party: A Marxist History* (Bookmarks, 1988), p63.

34 Berresford Ellis, as above, p36.

35 Challinor, as above, p187.

36 Maclean, as above, p135.

37 Gallacher, as above, p171.

38 Milton, as above, p9.

39 *Solidarity*, paper of the National Shop Stewards' and Workers' Committee Movement, February 1918.

40 Maclean, as above, p101.

41 Ripley and McHugh, as above, p108.

42 Quoted in Duncan Hallas, *The Meaning of Marxism* (Pluto Press, 1971), p35.

43 E H Carr, *The Bolshevik Revolution*, Volume 3 (Macmillan, 1953), p135.

44 Challinor, as above, p196.

45 Basil Thomson, *The Scene Changes* (Collins, 1939), p410.

46 *Times*, 30 January 1919.

47 Maclean, as above, p150.

48 Lord Shinwell, *I've Lived Through it All* (Gollancz, 1973), p37.

49 Andrew Rothstein, *The Soldiers' Strikes 1919* (Palgrave Macmillan, 1980), p94.

50 Rothstein, as above.

51 D S Morton, *The Forty Hours Strike* (SLP, 1919), p6.

52 *Glasgow Herald*, February 1919.

53 Gallacher, as above, p234.

54 Aneurin Bevan, *In Place of Fear* (Heinemann, 1952), p40.

55 Maclean, as above, p148.

56 Challinor, as above, p204.

57 *The Socialist*, 17 July, 1919.

58 Ripley and McHugh, as above, p175.

59 Ripley and McHugh, as above, p5.

60 McShane and Smith, as above, p150.

61 Maclean, as above, p220.

62 Trotsky's *Writings on Britain*, Volume 2 (New Park, 1975), p248.

63 Ripley and McHugh, as above, p174.

64 Maclean, as above, pp101, 114.